Best Roses

Stefan Buczacki
Best Roses

HAMLYN

Executive Art Editor Mark Richardson
Designer Wayne Theisinger, Town Group Consultancy
Editor Selina Higgins
Editorial Assistant Claire Musters
Production Heather O'Connell
Picture Research Jenny Faithfull

First published in Great Britain in 1996
by Hamlyn an imprint of Reed International books Limited
Michelin House, 81 Fulham Road, London SW3 6RB
and Auckland, Melbourne, Singapore and Toronto

Produced by Mandarin Offset, Singapore

ISBN 0 600 58340 6

A catalogue of this book is available at the British Library

CONTENTS

INTRODUCTION

No-one knows who first planted a rose in a garden or, indeed, who first recognised that roses stood out among wild flowering shrubs as something rather special. No-one knows who this first gardener was, but he or she was probably Chinese (although the Sumerians may have a rival claim) and lived something like 5,000 years ago. Since then, every civilization developing in areas where roses occur naturally (Europe, Asia, the Middle East and North America) has taken to their cultivation. No other flower has been so eulogised in music, literature and art. The question is, "why?".

I can't explain the extraordinary and enduring popularity of the rose where thousands of others have failed, but there can be no denying the special place that roses still have in the affections of gardeners around the world. Because of this, there was no doubting the choice of subject for the first book in my series to be devoted to a single type of plant.

But even that is misleading, for roses aren't 'a single type of plant'. There are around 100 species and goodness knows how many varieties; perhaps 10,000 have at some time existed.

Although I don't for a moment doubt the recent assertion that roses are no longer as popular as once they were and that considerably fewer are sold, I am also in no doubt that it is still the gardener's favourite flower. At least one can be found, so I'm told, in 80 per cent of British gardens.

I don't think the apparent decline in their popularity can have anything to do with roses themselves, for there have never been so many good, easy-to-grow, rewarding, long-flowering and colourful varieties available. It's simply that there are are now so many hundreds of other types of plant competing for our attention and our money.

My purpose here is to encourage ever more gardeners to grow ever more roses by introducing the wonderful range now available.

Roses climbing on a framework make a delightful feature in the garden

The beautiful maroon rosettes of the shrub rose 'Chianti' age to a deep crimson

TYPES OF ROSES

Roses are a very big group of garden plants and, although all require essentially the same growing conditions, there are many sub-divisions, each with their own characteristics. For some gardeners, the division into Old Roses and New Roses will be sufficient; for others the important distinction is between Bush Roses and Climbers; while for some, the only thing that really matters is the difference between a Hybrid Tea and a Floribunda. I've used a number of sub-divisions in the book and have described the important features of each in the Introductions to the various sections. There are certain general details, however, that are best clarified here. It must be said that, despite repeated attempts by International and National Rose Societies and rose breeders to impose standardization, very little has been accepted universally and no two rose growers or rose books will agree either on the names for different categories or their scope. I have adopted a system that I hope is based on common-sense and will be most useful to most people. But I don't pretend to have adhered to all of the rules.

By and large, the groupings that I have used are based on ancestry and breeding history and these generally dictate the really important flower and flowering characteristics, so you will find categories such as Damasks (p.48), Albas (p.50), Rugosas (p.52) and English Roses (p.76). But in addition to these groupings are others which describe the growth habit. For example, pretty well all of the older categories, by which I mean those roses that originated or were bred before around 1920, are shrubs and like most other flowering garden shrubs, they require relatively little pruning. There are also more recently bred roses of this type, unsurprisingly called Modern Shrub Roses (p.72). But, the Modern Shrub Rose group aside, most other modern roses soon become unkempt and unattractive if they are treated as shrubs. They tend to be smaller plants and are rather precisely pruned each year to keep them this way. These roses are usually called Bush Roses and are divided most importantly into Hybrid Teas (p.96) and Floribundas (p.84). Even smaller forms exist among some roses, especially some of the modern types, and I have grouped all of these little plants together as Miniatures and Patio Roses (p.80). Some of the rose groups include climbing forms and I have generally included these with the corresponding Shrub or Bush Rose descriptions but there are also a few groups in which all of the varieties climb; the Modern Climbers (p.114) and the Ramblers (p.120) are the most important.

ROOTSTOCKS AND THEIR SIGNIFICANCE

In common with fruit trees and many other types of ornamental garden shrub, the rose plant that you buy will usually comprise two separate varieties: a flowering variety grafted on to a rootstock variety. To be more precise, the term 'budded' rather than grafted is generally used with roses because the graft itself comprises a single bud, inserted into a slit in the bark of the rootstock variety. The reasons for this apparently complicated process are simple: it enables the rose nursery very rapidly to produce thousands of plants for sale (think of the number of buds on a single rose bush, each of which will make a new plant) and, most importantly, because the flowering varieties themselves do not tend to produce particularly strong or vigorous roots – they have, after all, been bred and selected for their flower quality.

Formerly, the Dog Rose, *Rosa canina* was used as a rootstock but better varieties have now been selected and most European rose nurseries use a form of the European species, *Rosa coriifolia*, popularly called 'Laxa' (its alternative species name is *Rosa laxa*), although others are used in different parts of the world. The use of 'Laxa' has partly overcome one of the inherent problems with any grafted plant, the production of suckers. These are shoots that arise from the roots and, being by definition generally more vigorous than the flowering variety, will soon 'take over'. 'Laxa' produces fewer suckers than *Rosa canina* but any found should be removed: scrape away the soil so that the point of origin on the root can be seen and tear the sucker away using strong gloves. If it is cut off, more suckers are likely to arise. Suckers can be distinguished by the difference in leaf-size: sucker leaves can be larger or smaller than those of the flowering variety.

STANDARDS

Budding onto rootstock varieties also allows the production of roses in the form of small trees, known as Standards. The rootstocks generally used for this in Europe are *Rosa rugosa* or a form of *Rosa canina* both of which readily produce the strong vertical stems needed. The traditional Standard has the flowering variety budded at a height of around 1m (3ft), while Half-standards are budded at about 80cm (32in) and Quarter-standards at 45cm (18in). The latter are generally grown as pot plants (see p.80). In theory, almost any rose variety can be budded and grown as a Standard, but some are much more suitable than others by virtue of their neat, bushy habit, vigour, weather tolerance and other features. The best are generally taken from among Floribundas and Hybrid Teas, most Shrub Roses being too vigorous. One particularly attractive version is the weeping Standard, generally budded at 1.5m (5ft) and comprising a Rambler, Ground-cover Rose or less vigorous flexible-stemmed Shrub Rose, the effect being that of a small weeping tree. They can be truly lovely and I have a weeping Standard formed from 'Canary Bird' (p.38) which is one of the joys of my garden in spring. While Standards aren't to everyone's taste, they are certainly an essential part of any formal flower garden.

THE NAMES OF ROSES

Apart from the Species Roses (p.32) that are grown more or less in their unaltered, wild form, all of the roses described in this book have been selected or bred for particular characteristics. The parentage and, in some instances, the more distant ancestry of roses is a fascinating subject which gives a wonderful insight into the way the garden rose has developed and the source of particular characteristics. In most instances, therefore, I have given the date of introduction and a brief note of the parentage of each variety, in so far as it is known, and as far as possible with credit to the breeder responsible. In a surprising number of cases, however, outstanding varieties have arisen from chance seedlings of unknown parentage while, also surprisingly, several breeders seem not to have recorded the crosses that resulted in particular successes. With a few Modern Roses the parentage has simply not been disclosed by the breeder.

Some rose varieties have more than one name and I have listed these synonyms, which are often simply translations to make the variety meaningful internationally: 'Snow Dwarf' and 'Schneezwerg' is an obvious example. In recent years, other peculiar names such as 'Auscountry', 'Fryclimbdown' and 'Kormalda' have appeared in some rose catalogues. These are trial ground names, little more than codes that enable the breeders of potential new varieties to be identified during their evaluation. They are invariably replaced with something more appealing once the new variety is marketed. They are of little interest or value to gardeners and I have not included them.

AWARDS

The world's leading national rose societies, as well as the Royal Horticultural Society, conduct trials and evaluations of new varieties every year, score them for flowering, disease resistance and other characteristics and grant various awards of merit. There are now so many of these that I haven't included them, although no rose that has picked up important distinctions will be omitted from the book. I have made an exception, however, in indicating those roses that have collected the important Rose of the Year Award, introduced in 1982 by British rose breeders.

Two contrasting climbing roses: the Rambler 'Chaplin's Pink Climber' and the climbing Hybrid Musk, 'Paul's Himalayan Musk'

HOW TO USE THE VARIETY ENTRIES

Inevitably, the selection of varieties to include in *Best Roses* has been a highly personal one. At any one time, around 2,500 rose species and varieties are available to the public and each year new ones are added while some are dropped. This book contains descriptions and comments on about 400, chosen for their appeal to me, their overall popularity and/or their availability. I haven't grown them all (although in the process of writing this book, I have surprised myself at just how many I have had personal experience of over the years), but I am familiar with each and every one. And I freely admit that I don't like some of the roses that I have included but I know that others do and that they are good varieties.

Those that I believe to be the most important have full entries; the remainder are grouped as 'Other Recomended Roses'. For all varieties, I've given basic information to help you make your own selections but to avoid repetition, I have abbreviated some details as follows:

FORM

An indication of height is given as follows:
All except Climbing Roses (and Ground Cover Roses see p.78) :
Miniature – up to 45cm (18in)
Small – from 45cm to 1.2m (18in to 4ft)
Medium-sized – from 1.2m to 2.5m (18in to 8ft)
Tall – above 2.5m (8ft)
Climbing Roses
Low – up to 2.5m (8ft)
Medium – 2.5m to 4m (8ft to 13ft)
Tall – above 4m (13ft)

FLOWERS

Single flowers have few petals, less than eight and often only five, with a mass of stamens in the centre. **Double** flowers have most of the stamens 'converted' into petals, although the degree of doubling varies from around 20 petals to 50 or more. Those with many petals are often called fully-double but I haven't attempted to categorize every variety in its degree of doubling which, in any event, can vary with growing conditions. **Semi-double** flowers have between about eight and 20 petals and almost always have some stamens visible in the centre.

The Modern Shrub, 'Fritz Nobis' is laden with delicate pink, semi-double blooms that appear in early summer

I have given some indications of flower **shape** but haven't tried to be very precise as the category can give a misleading impression; for every rose flower opens out and changes its shape enormously as it ages.

The appeal of a particular flower **colour** is in the eye of the beholder and again, especially with varieties that aren't illustrated, I've tried simply to help you make choices rather than to provide an encylopaedic definition. A precise colour description must be provided by raisers of new varieties but I haven't even adhered to these where I find them misleading. And, of course, as with shape, the colour of rose flowers may change greatly as they age.

Perfume or **fragrance** is perhaps the most controversial subject in all of rose growing. It's unarguable that most gardeners would prefer their roses to be fragrant and that, proportionately, more of the older than the modern varieties possess it to a significant degree. It is usually self-evident if a variety has slight, medium or strong fragrance and this is what I have indicated. But to categorize fragrance in such a personal way as to call it 'fruity', 'heavy' and so forth would, I'm sure, serve to steer gardeners away from varieties which on personal encounter would create a different impression. For this reason, I have avoided doing so, providing only basic information.

Flowering **period** is a matter of great importance to any gardener, and the fact that most of the older rose varieties produce most of their flowers in one glorious burst in early summer sets them apart from the much longer flowering period of most modern types. In indicating flowering time, therefore, I've distinguished between *spring-* or *summer-flowering* types and those that have *repeat-* or *continuous*-flowering characteristics. In practice, although a repeat-flowering rose may do as its name suggests, and flower in early and late summer, I find the distinction between this and continuous flowering to be blurred and due as much to particular seasons and weather as anything inherent.

HIPS

Although roses are grown primarily for their flowers, the fruits or **hips** can provide a bonus of interest towards the autumn and, where they are an important feature in any particular group, I've included a description of them. Of course, hips will be formed only when seed is set; and as seed-set requires

The autumn display of *Rosa moyesii*

pollen and stamens, it is the roses with single flowers that are the most reliable producers of good hips.

SPECIAL FEATURES

In this category I've singled out anything worthy of special remark, such as foliage appearance and colour or, most importantly, disease resistance.

SHADE TOLERANCE

The ability of roses to tolerate some degree of shade is important when siting them in gardens; and in gardens that are more or less permanently shaded, it will dictate which varieties can be grown. But I must emphasise that in my experience, no rose will tolerate really deep shade; or at least, will not produce attractive and worthy flowers in deep shade. Some, however, will thrive and produce perfectly acceptable results in gardens where there is some shading, and I've drawn attention to them. I've

used the designations for relative shade that I introduced in Book 3 of this series, *Best Shade Plants*, as follows. Imagine a walk from the edge of wood, where the shade will be **slight**, beneath the first trees, where it will be **moderate**, to the centre of the wood where it will be **deep**. Or, alternatively, in a garden that is shaded for part of the day, shade for half the morning would constitute slight; shade for half the day, moderate; and shade for almost the whole day would be described as deep.

WEATHER TOLERANCE

Generally, the ability of roses to tolerate weather isn't a matter of hardiness, for almost all of those I have described would be classified as very hardy, able to tolerate -20°C or below (-4°F or below). A few choice varieties will give of their best only in slightly milder areas, while several more will benefit from some protection from cold and drying winds and I've indicated where this is the case. But more important is the ability of the flowers to tolerate rain and this is the feature on which I have concentrated. By and large, the bigger the flower, the more likely it is to act as a sponge and be damaged by rain although relative thickness of the petals can also be a factor. Another important detail is the stage of flower development at which the rain falls, as many varieties are prone to balling in which the half-opened flower soaks up rain, begins to rot and, in consequence, never opens properly.

PRUNING

In all of the entries, pruning is indicated simply by a number and you should refer to the account of different pruning methods on pp.22–25 for further details.

HOW TO USE ROSES IN YOUR GARDEN

This heading may seem unduly didactic and, naturally, you are welcome to use roses in your garden in whichever way you choose; I hope, nonetheless, that a few suggestions may help. I suppose when garden roses are mentioned, the notion of the 'rose bed' first springs to mind: a bed or border where roses are grown to the exclusion of pretty well everything else. In many ways, I feel this style of planting has been the rose's undoing and the reason for the decline in its popularity. While a bed of roses, especially of repeat- or continuous-flowering varieties, should be very attractive during the summer, it can be extremely bleak for the rest of the year; and in a cold winter, when most roses lose all of their leaves, it can simply be a collection of twigs. In a large garden this may not matter, for other things can take your eye, but in a small garden the bleakness will dominate.

Early summer in my own Shrub Rose bed: *Rosa x richardii* in the fore-ground with the rich red of 'F J Grootendoorst' behind

I wish that more gardeners were willing to use roses in the same way as other flowering shrubs and interplant them in ornamental borders with herbaceous perennials (hardy geraniums and roses often make a particularly pleasing combination, see opposite), other shrubs, bulbs and even annuals. Roses also mix remarkably well with vegetables, fruit and herbs; I think I have almost as many roses dotted around my kitchen garden as I do in the ornamental areas. Roses are also used far too infrequently as individual specimens and, while most Hybrid Tea and Floribunda varieties may not work very well in this way, many of the larger Shrub Rose varieties can make superb centre-pieces or focal points.

Climbing Roses offer special opportunities for creativity and while the notion of having climbers festooned over your house in traditional cottage garden style might be appealing, it may not, in reality, be the best way of using them. If your house, like most houses, isn't a real cottage, a Climbing Rose, especially a fairly stiff-stemmed modern variety, trained on to a rigid trellis against the wall can look extremely artificial. And Climbing Roses trained on a wall will always be more prone to mildew because of the warmth and dryness of the situation. To help prevent this, the trellis or other support should be fixed to battens to lift it from the surface of the wall permitting as much air ciculation as possible. But there are far more natural-looking ways of displaying Climbers. Open structures, such as trellises, are perfect and arch-ways also make ideal supports for Climbing Roses and could be used in gardens far more: to form the entrance to a part of the garden or to frame a view. I think of pergolas as grander versions of archways, and although in large gardens, their uprights are often made of brick, in domestic situations wooden posts are perfectly adequate. As always, however, the timber must be pressure-treated with non-toxic preservative.

One of the most useful yet under-used supports for roses is the pillar, which is simply a post, old tree trunk (preferably not still on its own roots) or similar structure approximately 2m (6ft) tall, on and around which a relatively low-growing Climber is trained. A rose trained in this way makes an ideal feature. Living trees can also provide excellent supports for Climbing Roses, especially Climbers with more pliable stems. The larger and stronger the tree, the more vigorous the rose that may be grown over it, although I would advise using only strong old trees, whether large or small, for the purpose. Young trees may easily be weakened by having to support such extensive additional weight.

Just as Shrub or Bush Roses can be interplanted with other types of plant, so Climbing Roses can be used with other climbers, although the options are much more limited. Indeed, I would go so far as to recommend combining them only with clematis, chosen in colours to complement those of the roses and of a form and habit that won't result in mutual strangulation. It is important to choose those smaller-flowered clematis that flower from mid-summer onwards and thus require hard pruning. They can then be cut back at the same time as any rose pruning is performed in the early spring. Particularly suitable types of clematis are the varieties derived from *Clematis viticella* but a wide range of suggestions is included in Book 1 of this series, *Best Climbers*.

ROSES IN CONTAINERS

I have said on many occasions that any plant *can* be grown in a container (see Book 8 of this series, *Best Container Plants*). But it is important to establish how easily it can be done and if the time, effort, and cost involved is well enough repaid. With most roses, I don't think that it is, principally because roses have a high demand for water and develop deep roots to reach moisture reserves in the soil. A container for a rose, therefore, must be relatively deep in relation to its width and attention must be paid to watering. Nonetheless, I accept that there are people who adore roses and yet have no true garden and for whom growing their favourites in containers on a paved surface or balcony is the only available option. For them, I would suggest the following guidelines.

You really will make a rod for your own back if you try to grow any of the larger types of roses in containers, be they old or modern varieties but you will gain much pleasure and satisfaction from

some of the Miniature and Patio Roses (p.80). I now grow all of my Miniature Roses in containers from choice, for I find their diminutive features are shown to best advantage in this way. I use 20cm (8in) diameter terracotta pots, as I have always found terracotta to be much the best, affording the correct balance of moisture-retention and aeration that rose roots seem to need. I don't, however, advise using anything smaller. I use a high-quality soil-based potting compost (John Innes No. 3), apply a surface mulch of coarsely sieved garden compost, give water regularly during the summer and am assiduous in feeding twice a year (p.16). The roses are placed in full sun when they are in flower but moved into very light shade after each flush of flowers has faded.

INDOOR ROSES

Increasingly, you will see for sale in garden centres and by mail-order, a small range of tiny roses to be used as pot plants for indoor growing. These are Miniature varieties that have been raised by micropropagation (p.20). They have a certain charm and bring a little taste of rose growing to those whose garden may be no more than a windowsill. I have tried to condition these roses to outdoor growing after transferring them to more durable containers, but with limited success. They are seldom very hardy and invariably suffer from drying out unless kept in partial shade, but then they flower less than adequately. I think that they should be kept as house plants, although transferred after the first season to an attractive terracotta pot.

A delightful combination of roses, geraniums and poppies in the border

SOIL AND SITE

One of the things I am most frequently asked is to suggest plants that will be successful on clay soils. Invariably, roses feature prominently on my list, as their ability to flourish under such conditions is almost legendary in gardening. Unfortunately, this has led to a belief that roses will grow well only in a clay soil. It's important to understand, therefore, that there is nothing intrinsically special about clay; it is simply that a soil with a high clay content has good moisture-retentiveness and, as far as roses are concerned, this is what really matters. There are exceptions to this rule, however, for some fine and lovely roses – the beautiful single flowered 'Dunwich Rose' (below) springs immediately to mind – grow naturally on the sandy sea coast. Nonetheless, a moisture-retentive soil will enable all types of rose to thrive in your garden; including those derived from species that, in the wild, may be content in fairly free-draining sand.

The gravel walk in my own garden with a mound of 'Dunwich Rose' and the climbing form of 'Pompon de Paris' tumbling from an archway

There is one ingredient that a good rose soil needs above all others, and it should be added to your rose garden whatever its soil type: organic matter in the form of manure, compost or whatever is available. Spongy organic substances, rich in natural glue-like gels, will help to bind loose particles of a sandy soil to create moisture-retaining crumbs. But, paradoxically, it will also be of value in a heavy moist clay for it will help to prevent it from becoming *too* wet in winter and from drying out in the summer. The organic matter helps to form the crumbs and also the drainage pores between them, so creating a balance between too wet and too dry a soil.

If you intend to plant an entire rose bed, I strongly recommend **double digging**. This involves digging to two spades' depth by trenching across the plot and forking in organic matter as each trench is refilled with soil from the adjoining trench. Ideally, this is done around six months in advance of planting. If you are planting individual roses in established beds and borders, then organic matter is still important as I explain on page 18. But even after planting, the business is not finished for it is at least as important to continue adding organic matter, not by digging it in but by laying it on the surface as a mulch, up

'Dance du feu' will tolerate moderate to almost deep shade

(calcium carbonate) and add it at the rate recommended by the manufacturers for your existing soil pH and type (a chart is commonly provided on the packet). At higher pH levels (higher alkalinity), less can be done. It may be possible to lower the pH slightly using sulphur chips but you must expect some leaf yellowing in such soils and be prepared each spring to add a fertilizer containing sequestered iron to facilitate chlorophyll formation.

SITE

By choosing appropriate varieties, you can grow roses in most parts of your garden. It's probably fair to say that almost all roses will perform better in full sun, although the colour of some of the modern varieties does fade rather unattractively. No roses will tolerate deep shade but many will be successful in moderately shady spots and I have indicated relative shade-tolerance in my descriptions of individual varieties. Climbing Roses will almost inevitably experience more sheltered conditions than bush or shrub varieties. This has consequences for some pest and disease problems but also means that the soil will probably be drier. It is particularly important, therefore, to prepare the site very thoroughly for Climbing Roses and then mulch it regularly.

The relative exposure of your garden is also a factor that must be taken into account when choosing roses. They vary in what is generally called their weather tolerance, which really means the likelihood of the flowers suffering damage by rain and of the foliage being browned by winds. I have given an indication of weather tolerance from my own experience in the individual descriptions, but in really very exposed

to 10 or 15cm (4 or 6in) deep around and between your roses. This should be done twice a year, in late autumn and then in early spring, immediately after the first feeding (p.16). The surface mulch will help retain soil moisture (and also suppress some weeds) before it is slowly dragged down by worms and incorporated in the body of the soil to improve the overall structure.

The pH of the soil (its relative acidity or alkalinity) isn't especially critical with roses, provided it isn't extreme. The pH can be checked with tolerable accuracy using a small testing kit and, between about pH 5.5 and pH 7.5, few problems should be experienced. At lower pH levels (higher acidity), however, it will be beneficial to add lime to the soil in autumn. Use garden lime

SOIL AND SITE

gardens, you will generally fare best of all with the Rugosas (p.52), some of the Species Roses and, often, some of the varieties with small single flowers. The Tea Roses (p.67) as a group are bit on the tender side and, as you might expect, varieties with huge flowers which act like sponges suffer badly in the rain.

FOOD AND WATER

No plant will grow without food and water but while wild roses will find all of their needs fulfilled in the soil, rather more is required by our garden varieties. This is partly because we expect better quality growth than is acceptable in the wild but also because varieties that have been artificially selected and bred for flower and other qualities have inherently higher demands, especially for nutrients. Fortunately, the needs are easily satisfied by supplementary feeding with a fertilizer, and rose feeding is neither expensive nor complicated. Before giving my recommendations, however, it will help to outline the essential features of an appropriate fertilizer.

The main plant nutrients are nitrogen (N), the most important of all nutrients, which encourages the growth of leaves; phosphorus (P), which is especially important for roots, and potassium (K), which is significant for the development of flowers and fruit.

Although each type of plant has its own specific needs, most garden plants, including roses, will fare pretty well with a small handful twice a season of a fertilizer that contains approximately equal amounts of the three major nutrients. There are both artificial and organically based fertilizers that will supply these perfectly adequately. Growmore is a well known balanced artificial fertilizer with 7 per cent each of N, P and K (designated on the packet

as 7:7:7). Fish, blood and bone is an organically based equivalent with an N:P:K ratio of around 5:5:6. But with a little more thought, it is not difficult to do even better.

As flowering plants, roses have a need for proportionately more potash than plants grown simply for their foliage, so a fertilizer with a bias towards potash is more valuable. But plants need minor as well as the three major nutrients and, although it is relatively rare for British soils to be deficient in any of these, plants can sometimes have difficulty in absorbing them. In alkaline (chalky) soils especially, the uptake of iron, which is important for the manufacture of the green pigment chlorophyll, is impaired for many plants, including roses. The obvious result is that leaves become yellowed with contrasting green veins but the more important effect is that the plant as a whole functions less than satisfactorily. For this reason, specific formulations of rose fertilizers have been devised over the years that take account of these needs, and both artificially and organically based rose blends are now available. My recommendation is that one of these specific, proprietary rose fertilizers be applied twice each season; first immediately after the spring pruning and then again as the first flush of flowers begins to fade in early summer. Additionally, I strongly recommend using bonemeal, a fertilizer particularly rich in phosphorus, when planting new roses (see p.18) as it encourages the all-important vigorous root development which, in turn, ensures good nutrient uptake from the soil and firm anchorage.

For those who garden on alkaline soils (above pH 7), I recommend the use of a special fertilizer containing sequestered

iron in addition to the twice-yearly application of bonemeal in early spring and autumn. Sequestered iron is iron in an organic form, readily absorbed by plants and it is important because in such strongly alkaline conditions, even the iron provided by specific rose fertilizers may be taken up inadequately. A sequestered iron fertilizer should be applied once a year in early spring.

Foliar feeding with liquid fertilizers has become popular for many types of garden plant in recent years. It capitalizes on the fact that plants can take up relatively small amounts of nutrient through their leaves as well as through their roots, and that in this way the nutrient enters the tissues more rapidly. It has some merits for very rapidly growing plants, especially annuals, during the summer but I find it has no particular value with roses which, in any event, have thick, rather waxy leaf surfaces which readily reject liquids.

While roses have fairly high water demands, they can generally satisfy their needs by virtue of their deep roots, tapping into water reserves deep within the soil. Newly planted roses, however, will need additional watering during their first season and Climbing Roses, growing in inherently dry conditions close to walls or other supports, will always benefit from additional water. In more free-draining soils too, additional water will be necessary but all roses must be heavily mulched twice each season, in spring and in autumn. The best mulching material for roses is well-rotted stable manure, with farmyard manure and compost good alternatives, but they should be applied at least 5cm (2in) thick and always onto soil that is already moist. Mulching a dry soil will simply help to keep it dry

The soil around this semi-double climber must be mulched regularly and should not be allowed to dry out

CHOOSING AND PLANTING ROSES

To be sure that your roses give you the best possible return for your investment you must obtain them from a reputable supplier and plant them carefully.

CHOOSING

Roses can be bought in one of two ways: by mail-order from a rose grower, or by personal shopping at a nursery or garden centre. There are advantages and disadvantges to both. Buying by mail-order will give you by far the widest choice of plants and, indeed, will be the only way of obtaining many of the varieties that I recommend. As you are unable to see the plants before purchase, you will be in the hands of the supplier in respect of plant quality, but it would be surprising if a British rose nursery let you down. Mail-order plants will usually be sent only when the plants are dormant, during the autumn and spring, for they are normally dispatched bare-rooted. Occasionally, container-grown plants in growth may be mailed but this is a risky and costly business.

Personal shopping will allow you to see the plants and will also mean that you can buy container-grown stock for planting at any time of the year, although spring or autumn are still best. But only the most popular varieties will be offered. Perhaps the best compromise is to make a summer visit to the rose fields of one of the major national growers, make your selection from a huge range and place your order for delivery later in the season. A good-quality plant should normally have between three and five stems, each neatly pruned back to between 25 and 45cm (10 and 18in) in length and be well and uniformly furnished with main and fibrous roots. It should also be free from suckers (see p.8) which will weaken the whole plant. A common fault is that the rose is lop-sided with roots concentrated on one side only and plants like this should be avoided. Plants in containers should have compost to the level of, or just above, the graft point at the stem base; I still see far too many container roses that appear as if on stilts with the compost washed away from the roots. Finally, as with any container-grown plants, there should be little or no sign of moss- or weed-growth on the compost itself.

PLANTING

It's important to place Climbers 25cm (10in) from their support. Excavate a hole at least twice the volume of the spread roots of a bare-rooted plant or of the compost ball of a container-grown one. Lightly prune the roots of a bare-rooted plant to encourage fibrous root development and better establishment. Similarly, gently tease away the roots from around the compost ball of a container-grown plant to stimulate growth out into the soil. Fork well rotted manure or compost into the base of the planting hole with a handful of bonemeal and then spread the roots or position the compost ball in the hole and fill in around with a mixture of soil, more organic matter and bonemeal. With Standard or Half-standard Roses, hammer a stake 60cm (24in) into the soil and on the windward side of the stem so the plant is blown away from the stake. Move the plant up and down to eradicate air pockets and then firm in the soil. Lightly mound the soil around the base and ensure that the graft union is 2–3cm (1–1½in) below soil level. Standards and half-standards should then be secured to the stake. Finally, cut back shoots 15cm (6in) above soil level, or, with standards, to 15cm (6in) above the graft union at the top of the stem.

ROSE SICKNESS

One of the most important, if unexpected, factors that governs where and if roses should be planted is how recently other roses have been grown

Firm in the soil with your boot after planting

Newly delivered roses may be heeled in temporarily before planting

on the same site. If new roses are planted directly into soil from which older roses have been removed, the chances are that they won't establish well. The reason is a condition known as rose sickness or rose replant problem. No-one fully understands it but it seems that there is a build-up in the soil of a microscopic root-attacking fungus. It doesn't have much impact on the well established plants because it attacks only the tough old roots while new vigorous roots can push out into clean soil. When a new rose is placed in the same spot, however, its new young roots are vulnerable. There are three solutions: leave the plot free from roses for about three years (effective but very inconvenient), use container-grown plants (moderately effective but with the inevitably limited choice of varieties that this will mean) or replace the soil in each planting hole with soil from an area elsewhere in the garden that has not grown roses (overall, the best and most practical solution).

New growth in spring from a rose planted in the previous autumn

This climber has been planted about 25cm (10in) from its support to give the roots ample room to spread and provide secure anchorage

PROPAGATION

Raising your own plants and making more of those you have already is an integral part of gardening. But it is probably less true of roses than of any other important group of plants. Apart from the Species, there are very few types of rose that will come true from seed and, although many worthy varieties originated as seedlings from chance crosses, the likelihood of finding anything worthwhile by good fortune is remote. Even rose breeders, who make deliberate crosses between carefully chosen parents, have to grow hundreds of seedlings through to flowering size and then perform several years of testing in order to find a handful that are worth taking any further down the line of cultivation. It isn't something most gardeners would contemplate, but the process itself is not a difficult one to perform.

Hips should be collected in early winter when they are fully ripe, and the seeds carefully separated and washed away from the flesh. The dry seeds are then best stored in an airtight container, in a fridge and sown shallowly in early spring in a gritty, soil-based compost in a cold-frame. Germination should occur sporadically over a period of weeks during which time the young seedlings should be potted on, and they should flower within the first season.

It is unlikely that you will want to multiply the number of plants of any particular rose but it can be done simply by hardwood cuttings. Cut approximately 15–20cm (6–8in) lengths of the current year's healthy shoots in late autumn and trim them to just above a bud at the top and just below one at the bottom. Then insert the shoots into the soil in a sheltered part of the garden or in a cold-frame to approximately half their length. They should form roots within six or nine months but I find it best not to move the young plants until the following autumn. Modern roses, especially Hybrid Teas and Floribundas, strike less readily than older varieties and Species Roses. Most roses can also be layered. A low-growing shoot is pegged down into the soil, and ideally a rock or other weight placed on top. The shoot should produce roots within about 12 months, at which time it can be severed from the parent plant.

It's almost inevitable these days that gardeners will come across the term **micropropagation** (the tiny indoor roses that I mention on p.80 are all micropropagated) and although it is not really practical to do yourself, it is an interesting technique. Tiny fragments of living tissue are removed from a plant under carefully controlled aseptic conditions, placed onto a nutrient jelly and incubated. The tissue develops into a miniature plant which is then carefully transferred to a more conventional potting compost, the plant hardened off and offered for sale. It provides a ready method for the mass-production of small plants but there are other important features. The technique guarantees complete uniformity among the progeny and it also offers the grower the ability to produce plants free from virus contamination in their tissues. This is important for the health of the individual plants but, commercially, an even more significant factor is that it enables plants to be *guaranteed* healthy and thus allows them to be exported to countries with strict plant health regulations.

Collect seed from the large hips of 'Fru Dagmar Hastrup' in winter

Older rose varieties such as 'Alba Maxima' are especially easy to propagate from cuttings

PRUNING

If one task is synonymous with rose growing, that task is pruning, yet it still prompts more questions, poses gardeners with more uncertainty and is generally still imbued with the greatest mystery. The confusion is compounded because even very experienced rose growers disagree on the best methods to follow when pruning roses. Recently, there has even been a dispute over the need for careful pruning of any description, and a few good and worthy gardeners believe that 'pruning' modern roses with powered hedge-trimmers gives perfectly satisfactory results; so clearly, my advice won't satisfy everyone. I have, however, included the methods which work best for me, although I don't pretend that they are the only ones.

The Alba rose, 'Céleste' should be lightly pruned each year

Whatever the method, good pruning is only achieved with good tools and no rose grower can manage without a pair of secateurs or pruners. Choose between the single-bladed anvil pattern which is best for hard woody stems but tends to crush softer ones, and the two-bladed scissor or by-pass type, which is less robust but gentler in action. Ideally, have both. If you have large Shrub Roses or Climbers with very stout, woody stems, you will also require a pair of loppers which, in essence, are long-handled secateurs for thicker branches, and are also available in both anvil or by-pass style. You may occasionally need to resort to something stronger still, and a curved pruning saw may be necessary on really big and tough Shrub Roses. As with all garden tools, I can do no more than repeat the advice that I have given many times: buy the best that you can afford, although it is worth adding that the difference between good and poor quality cutting tools is more marked than with most other types of gardening aid.

Rose pruning isn't complicated and, although the different groups do require rather different pruning techniques if the plants are to give of their best, in every case the processes follow well established principles. Before I outline my recommendations, however, let's just look at those basic principles.

Pruning is the process of cutting off parts of plants. Clearly, this reduces their size but, more importantly, it stimulates other parts to grow, for the buds at the end, or apex of a stem exert a chemical suppressing influence on other buds further down. This phenomenon is called apical dominance. Cut off the end of a rose stem, therefore, and those other buds, freed of chemical constraints, will burst into life. If they are flower buds, you will have flowers further down the stem and very often, as with Climbing Roses, if you prune away the apex and then bend down the stem to the horizontal (which also helps to diminish apical dominance) this will stimulate flowering at the base of an otherwise fairly flowerless stem.

Cutting away a large proportion of a rose is called **hard pruning**; cutting away a little is called **light pruning**. In general, you should hard prune roses that are less vigorous growers simply because, as I've described, in stimulating bud development, pruning generates more growth. The harder you prune, the more vigorously the rose will grow in response and if you regularly hard prune a very vigorous rose such as the Floribunda 'The Queen Elizabeth', the more you will have to prune each year.

Regardless of the amount of stem to be removed, pruning cuts should always be made just above a bud, leaf, flower, branch fork or other actively growing structure, never in the middle of a stem or branch. This ensures that the cut surface heals quickly and doesn't merely wither and allow decay organisms to enter (which I'm sure must happen if you follow the hedge-trimmer technique). Except on very slender stems, the cut should be sloped away from the bud or other organ, but not so close as to damage it – about 5mm (¼in) above is generally safe. In so far as it is possible, cut back Shrub and Bush Roses (including Standards) to just above a bud that faces outwards, and Climbing and Rambling Roses to just above a bud that points upwards or in which ever other direction growth is needed to fill a gap.

As with everything else connected to rose growing, there are differing opinions on how far the old flowered shoots should be cut back but I stick with the traditional approach which has served me well: I cut back to just above the first leaflet with five, rather than three leaflets, and a strong outward-facing bud.

There always will be much argument about the timing of rose pruning; should it be done in autumn or spring? By and large, I don't prune in autumn. I find that in relatively cold areas, leaving on the old growth during the winter affords the plants more protection against hard frosts, which will kill off, in any event, some shoot growth. In mild areas, by contrast, autumn pruning can encourage soft new growth to develop during the winter, growth that is then prone to damage by frost and cold winds in spring. So the only autumn pruning that I do is the removal of abnormally long and whippy shoots on Climbing or Bush Roses which would otherwise be blown around by winter winds and thus physically moved and weakened in the soil. The only summer pruning, apart from deadheading, that I advocate is on Ramblers (see Methods 5 and 6).

To avoid repetition, I haven't given detailed pruning instructions under each rose entry; just a reference to Methods, which are numbered 1 to 8. Specific instructions follow:

METHOD 1

Use with: Species Roses, most of the groups of Shrub Roses including Moss Roses, Gallicas, Centifolias, Damasks, Albas, Rugosas, Hybrid Musks, some varieties of China Roses, Bourbons, Noisettes, Tea Roses, Modern Shrubs, Polyanthas, Hybrid Perpetuals and Ground-cover Roses.

Method 1

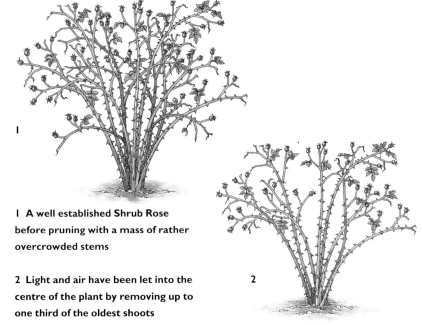

1

1 **A well established Shrub Rose before pruning with a mass of rather overcrowded stems**

2 **Light and air have been let into the centre of the plant by removing up to one third of the oldest shoots**

2

PRUNING

Very little pruning is needed. Each year, cut out any damaged, dying or diseased shoots to a few centimetres above soil level and every two or three years, cut out one or two of the largest, thickest and oldest shoots in order to encourage regular shoot renewal. It is sometimes suggested that some of the main shoots should be shortened each year but I strongly discourage this as it produces a proliferation of shoots from the point of the cut, giving a mop-head appearance. Deadhead the flowers if the plants are small enough to reach with ease but don't deadhead those varieties that produce attractive autumn hips.

METHOD 2
Use with: Floribundas, English Roses and larger Patio Roses
Each year, cut out any dead, damaged, feeble or dying shoots to a few centimetres above soil level. Then cut back, also to just above soil level, the oldest one-third of the shoots and finally, cut back the remaining shoots by one third of their length.

METHOD 3
Use with: Hybrid Teas
Each year, cut out any dead, damaged, feeble or dying shoots to a few centimetres above soil level. Then cut back all remaining shoots by approximately half of their length.

METHOD 4
Use with: Miniature Roses and smaller Patio Roses
The whole operation is best described as tidying up and should always be done in the spring, after the last hard frost. Cut back all dead and dying shoots (there will generally be a number of these) to just above soil level. Also thin out the overall number of shoots to eliminate congestion. Then cut back any long, old flowered shoots to approximately 10cm (4in) above the base of the plant, (many Miniatures produce flowering shoots at least double the height of the rest of the plant) and finally, cut back all remaining shoots by approximately one-third of their length.

METHOD 5
Use with: Wichuraiana Ramblers
When young, train the plants (see opposite) to form a framework. Then, each year, cut back up to one-third of the old stems to just above soil level after flowering and cut back the old flowered side-shoots on the remainder, to within about 10cm (4in) of their junction with the main stems.

METHOD 6
Use with: Multiflora Ramblers
When young, train the plants (see opposite) to form a framework, then for the next two or three years, cut back old flowered side-shoots after flowering to within about 10cm (4in) of their junction with the main stems. On older, established plants, cut back old flowered stems to soil level after flowering.

METHOD 7
Use with: Species Climbers, Modern Climbers, Hybrid Musk Climbers, Bourbon Climbers
Very little pruning is needed. When young, train the plants (see opposite) to form a framework. Then, each year, cut out any dead, dying, diseased or crossing shoots, tie in any vigorous new shoots, bending them as close as possible to the horizontal and cut out one or two old shoots each year, if sufficient new shoots are available to replace them as part of the main framework. If there are not enough new shoots, leave the main framework unpruned. After tying in, cut back any very long shoots to contain them within the available space.

Method 2

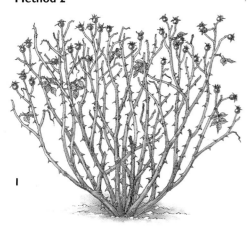

1

1 **A Floribunda at the end of its flowering season with a mass of overcrowded stems and dead flowered shoots**

2 **Dead and damaged stems have been removed and the remaining stems have been cut back by one third**

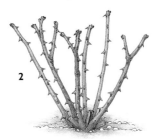

2

Method 3

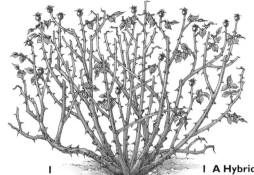

1

2

1 **A Hybrid Tea at the end of its flowering season with a mass of overcrowded stems and dead flowered shoots**

2 **Dead and damaged stems have been removed and all of the remaining stems have been cut back by half**

Pruning climbing roses

A Climbing rose showing the way in which the shoots have been trained horizontally to form a framework that covers the wall or other supporting structure. This should be done at an early age with all forms of Climbing and Rambling Roses

METHOD 8

Use with: Noisette Climbers, Hybrid Perpetual Climbers, Climbing Tea Roses, Climbing Hybrid Teas, Climbing Floribundas

When young, train the plants (see above) to form a framework. Then, each year, cut back the old flowered side-shoots to within 10-15cm (4-6in) of their junction with the main framework. Every few years, replace one or two old shoots in the framework if sufficient vigorous new shoots are available to take their place. If not, leave the main framework untouched.

PRUNING STANDARD ROSES

As I have explained (p.23), Standard Roses are simply shrub or bush varieties grafted onto rootstocks with a strong vertical stem. They should be pruned in the same way as their normal counterparts except that all pruning cuts are made relative to the head, the position where the flowering variety has been budded, where swelling will be apparent, not to soil level or the base of the plant.

DEADHEADING

Deadheading is the cutting away of the old flowered heads. This is partly for tidiness, but it also lessens the likelihood

Deadhead all roses by cutting back the dead flower head to a bud just above the first leaf that has five, rather than three leaflets

of diseases becoming established and encourages new buds to burst which with repeat- or continuous-flowering varieties, will result in a fresh flush of flowers later in the season. The only varieties that shouldn't be deadheaded are the Species and Shrub Roses that produce attractive hips in the autumn; and also, of course, those plants that are simply too big to manage.

PRUNING ROSE HEDGES

There is little point in growing roses as hedging plants if they are hard pruned or clipped in the same way as more formal hedges, for this will simply remove the flower buds. My advice, therefore, is to treat them as exactly what they are – a long line of flowering shrubs – and perform the minimum amount of pruning needed to keep them tidy. In many instances, almost no pruning will be required other than the removal of the occasional dead or feeble shoot.

PESTS AND DISEASES

Like all garden plants, roses are affected by a range of pests and diseases but mildew, blackspot and, to a lesser extent, rust, and several species of aphid (greenfly) outweigh all others in most gardens.

Most of the important rose diseases, including blackspot, rust and mildew, are caused by microscopic fungi, all of which require moisture for their spores to germinate and grow but, contrary to what is sometimes thought, not all require damp conditions thereafter. The most important exception to this is the type called powdery mildews. After their initial germination, these fungi thrive best in hot dry conditions, exactly the conditions in which most Climbing Roses like to grow. It is not surprising, therefore, that Climbing Roses as a group are especially prone to this particular disease.

There are no important bacterial diseases of roses but occasionally the effects of a virus may be seen. The symptoms are less definitive than those of fungal diseases and usually take the form of a yellowish leaf patterning, together with a crinkled or crumpled effect appearing on the leaves. Viruses can be introduced into rose tissues by sap-sucking pests such as aphids or by soil-inhabiting creatures such as eelworms (nematodes).

Roses have several animal pests: among the larger types, mammals, especially rabbits and deer can be damaging to roses in some areas but the biggest problems are likely to come from small pests, especially insects. All insects, of course, are cold-blooded and so their activity and reproductive rate both increase as the temperature rises. This is why they cause such problems for roses, particularly for those such as Climbers which grow in a sheltered site. Insect pests can be divided roughly into two groups: the chewing types such as caterpillars and slugworms that may be small in quantity but

One form of rose mosaic virus

are rather large in the effect they have, for they remove pieces of leaf and flower bodily and sap-sucking types, such as aphids, that achieve much of their impact through force of numbers, wearing down the plant's vigour.

Aphids on a rose bud

Damage to rose leaves caused by leaf-cutter bee

Leaf-rolling sawfly

Given this information about how rose pests and diseases thrive, what can be done to minimize their effects? Firstly, in an ideal world, we would select varieties that have natural resistance, at least to the major diseases. This would, however, greatly limit the number of roses available to chose from. Generally, it is true to say that proportionately more older roses are disease-prone, and certainly proportionately more yellow-flowered roses are susceptible to blackspot. With modern roses, disease susceptibility is an important consideration in evaluating new varieties, and one that scored badly in this respect would be unlikely to reach commercial production.

A second approach is to make the environment less attractive to the pests and diseases, but this is not easy because of the physical nature of the plants and the way we grow them. Nonetheless, growing Climbing Roses

Roses affected with blackspot will benefit from a hard pruning in spring

on a trellis in the open, over trees and shrubs, up pillars and in similar positions – in fact almost anywhere other than on a brick or stone wall – will help you ensure that there is some air movement around the plants and less incentive for both insects and spores to settle. When Climbing Roses are

grown on walls, ensure the support is raised a few centimetres away from the wall surface (see p.12) to allow air circulation *behind* the plants. You can help to create a moist environment around the plants and also confer other benefits, by first ensuring that the soil is thoroughly moist, and then mulching

PESTS AND DISEASES

Coarse, pale spotting caused by the leafhopper which feeds on the underneath of the leaves and leaps from the plant when disturbed

Yellowing between the veins of the leaves is caused by an iron or other trace element shortage in alkaline soils with a high organic content

with organic matter around the base. Growing roses as more or less isolated individuals (see p.12) rather than massed together, where a problem can hop easily from one plant to the next, will also be less favourable for both pests and diseases.

The third line of defence is to keep a weather-eye open for the initial signs of attack early on in the season and then physically pinch off the problem. But the simple removal of affected areas is seldom the complete answer. If the problem is a recurring one, then more direct action is needed and it is in these cases that personal choice becomes an important factor.

CHEMICAL CONTROL OF PESTS AND DISEASE

Every modern gardener will realize that over-use of chemicals in the garden will cause harm to the environment. Very few chemicals can discriminate between good and harmful insects, some have unfortunate side-effects on other organisms (some insecticides, for example, are very harmful to fish) and yet others may persist in the soil with rather uncertain long-term consequences. It's worth remembering that these effects are every bit as likely to occur with so-called natural or organic products as they are with artificial ones. So I advise using chemicals of any type in moderation, and use them as the last not the first option and, of course, use them only in the manner and at the doses that the manufacturers indicate. If you do have recourse to a chemical spray, however, it's always worth using a combined pesticide and fungicide which will combat the major problems in a single operation, so saving you both time and money.

In recent seasons, an increasing number of biological controls has become available to gardeners and more will undoubtedly do so in years to come. Unfortunately, they are of very limited value to the rose grower because there are no biological controls for diseases, only for pests, and those currently most effective are for use in greenhouses or against soil-inhabiting pests which are not, by and large, the ones that cause the biggest problems on roses.

In the charts that follow, I have given a key to the problems most likely to be found on Roses, offered my suggested treatments and listed the most common and important garden fungicides and insecticides. I have also described the effects of the few instances of fertilizer-deficiency that you are likely to encounter.

Yellow and black pustules on the upper-leaf surface are caused by rust

The presence of mildew can often result in leaf death and affected plants should be sprayed

PESTS AND DISEASES

IDENTIFICATION OF COMMON ROSE PEST, DISEASE AND DEFICIENCY PROBLEMS

SYMPTOMS ON LEAVES	CAUSE
Irregular holes; pieces removed	Caterpillars
Infested with green, pink or brown insects	Aphids
Sticky or black-sooty deposit	Aphids
Small irregular holes, especially at shoot tips	Capsid bugs
Fine whitish mottling	Leafhoppers
Regular, semi-circular pieces removed from edges	Leaf-cutter bees
Surface eroded away, small greenish larvae present	Slug sawflies (slugworms)
Leaflets rolled tightly and drooping	Leaf-rolling sawflies
Discoloured, bronzed or yellow, may be shrivelled	Red spider mites
Powdery white coating	Powdery mildew
Dark brown-black blotches; no mould (common)	Blackspot
Small dark, brown-black blotches; mould on undersides (uncommon)	Downy mildew
Tiny, powdery orange pustules	Rust
Tiny, powdery yellow or black pustules on undersides	Rust
Irregular yellow streaks and patterns	Virus
Small irregular brownish spots	Leaf spots
Bleached, with veins dark green	Iron deficiency
Wilting, with no other symptoms	Wilt
Silvery sheen	Silver leaf

SYMPTOMS ON BUDS AND PART OPENED FLOWERS	CAUSE
Irregular holes; pieces removed	Caterpillars
Infested with green, pink or brown insects	Aphids
Tiny, powdery orange pustules	Rust
Shrivelled, with fluffy grey mould	Botrytis
Forming compact ball and failing to open	Rain followed by botrytis

SYMPTOMS ON FLOWERS	CAUSE
Irregular holes; pieces removed	Caterpillars
Infested with green, pink or brown insects	Aphids
Tiny, powdery orange pustules	Rust
Powdery white coating	Powdery mildew
Shrivelled, with fluffy grey mould	Botrytis grey mould
Fine, pale flecks; tiny elongated insects present	Thrips

SYMPTOMS ON SHOOTS AND STEMS	CAUSE
Infested with green, pink or brown wingless insects	Aphids
Multiple shoots arise from buds	Late frost
Canker lesions and/or dying-back	Cankers or botrytis
Hard, irregular swelling at soil (not to be confused with normal swelling around graft)	Crown gall
Bright, fluffy red-orange growth ('robin's pincushion') mainly on Species and Wild Roses	Gall wasp

TREATMENT OF ROSE PEST, DISEASE AND DEFICIENCY PROBLEMS

PROBLEM	TREATMENT
Aphids	Spray with contact or systemic insecticide
Blackspot	Spray with systemic fungicide or sulphur; apply tar oil spray in winter and prune hard in spring
Botrytis grey mould	Spray with systemic fungicide or sulphur
Cankers	Cut out damaged stems
Capsid bugs	Insects are too erratic in occurrence to make treatment feasible

PROBLEM	TREATMENT
Caterpillars	If insects are seen, spray with contact insecticide or bacterial spray
Crown gall	No treatment necessary unless plant is very severely affected when it should be dug up and destroyed
Downy mildew	Spray with fungicide containing copper oxychloride
Gall wasp	Cut out affected part if disfiguring
Iron deficiency	Apply sequestered iron fertilizer (see p.16)
Leaf-cutter bees	Insects are too erratic in occurrence to make treatment feasible
Leafhoppers	Insects are too erratic in occurrence to make treatment feasible
Leaf-rolling sawfly	Insects are too erratic in occurrence to make treatment feasible
Leaf spots	If severe, spray with systemic fungicide
Powdery mildew	Spray with systemic fungicide or sulphur
Red spider mites	Mulch heavily, try to ensure that plant doesn't dry out and if necessary, move to a more sheltered, less hot and dry position
Rust	Spray with fungicide containing penconazole or myclobutanil
Silver leaf	Dig up and destroy plant
Slug sawflies	If insects are seen, spray with contact insecticide
Thrips	If insects are seen, spray with contact or systemic insecticide
Wilt	Dig up and destroy plant
Virus	No treatment necessary unless severe, when plant should be dug up and destroyed

SOME FUNGICIDES, INSECTICIDES AND OTHER PESTICIDAL TREATMENTS FOR ROSE PROBLEMS

FUNGICIDES	USES AND COMMENTS
Carbendazim	Systemic, for most foliage and stem diseases, including powdery mildew and grey mould
Mychobutanil	Systemic, especially useful for leaf spots and rust
Penconazole	Systemic, especially useful for leaf spots and rust
Triforine	Systemic, for powdery mildew and other foliage diseases
Copper oxychloride*	Non-systemic, for some leaf spots and downy mildew
Sulphur*	Non-systemic, for powdery mildew and other foliage diseases

Note: It should be noted that some of these chemicals are only available in particular formulations or in combination with certain other chemicals. Some may also be marketed for specific pest or disease problems only. In every case, you must read the label directions carefully to be sure that the product is being used for the purpose and in the manner for which it is intended. The names given above are those of the active chemical ingredients. These will not be the same as the product brand names, but will be found printed on the product label.

INSECTICIDES	USES AND COMMENTS
Dimethoate	Systemic, most pests
Derris (rotenone)*	Contact, most pests
Horticultural soaps	Contact, most pests
Malathion	Contact, most pests
Permethrin	Contact, most pests
Pirimicarb	Contact, specific to aphids
Pyrethrum*	Contact, most pests
Tar oil	Contact, use in dormant season only against overwintering pests; also of limited value against blackspot

OTHER PRODUCTS	USES AND COMMENTS
Bacterial spray*	Contact caterpillars

*Generally acceptable to organic gardeners

Systemic substances are absorbed by the plant and require less frequent and less accurate spraying than contact materials

SPECIES AND NEAR-SPECIES

On the face of it, most species roses appear to lack many of the features that gardeners have come to expect and look for in their garden plants. They tend to have small, single flowers with little fragrance and a short blooming period. You can readily see just why people have crossed and selected them to produce more imposing garden varieties and yet, for me and many other gardeners, several of them do have an undeniable charm. They are well worth growing if you have room but I have to admit that in a small garden, where a long flowering season is desirable, they can barely be considered to earn their keep.

I've included in this selection a few plants that I call near-species; they differ relatively little from the wild forms to which they are related and while some are the results of deliberate crosses, others have arisen as chance seedlings found growing close to the species parent, the pollen having come from goodness knows where.

Rosa biebersteinii (syn. *Rosa horrida*)

❝ *I first grew this plant when it was called* Rosa horrida *and that name alone was enough to put off plenty of my fellow gardeners. It originates from eastern Europe and western Asia but has never excited much enthusiasm and I've even seen it described as being no better than a gooseberry, which is singularly unfair. In reality,* horrida *only means prickly which is a reasonable description although I don't know that it's any more prickly than many another species. I still grow it because I like its small flowers which have a cream hint to them* rather than being pure white, and its pretty little red hips. And I find it sits well in a mixed border where it blends into the general run of things when not in flower. ❞

Rosa biebersteinii

FORM
Small, bushy shrub.
FLOWERS
Single, cream-white, with a slight fragrance, summer.
HIPS
Small, red.
SPECIAL FEATURES
Leaves unusual, small, greyish-green.

SHADE TOLERANCE None to light.
WEATHER TOLERANCE Moderate.
PRUNING – 1

Rosa canina

❝ *The name* canina *suggests something to do with dogs, although what I cannot tell, save that this plant has for centuries been known as the dog rose. Perhaps 'dog' is being used in the sense of something common and base, for this is most certainly the commonest and most familiar of all native British and European roses and in many parts of the country there is scarcely a hedgerow that doesn't contain a good growth of it. It achieved its merit as a garden plant through being used as the rootstock onto which grander roses were budded. That role is now taken by another European rose,* Rosa coriifolia *(generally called 'Laxa') but I see no reason why the dog rose shouldn't be planted in its own right in wilder gardens. Raising it from seed can be rewarding for it is probably the most variable of all rose species and you never know what you will produce.* ❞

FORM
Tall, rather lax shrub.
FLOWERS
Single, very variable in colour, generally pink but sometimes almost red and occasionally white, moderately fragrant, flowers in summer.
HIPS
Medium-sized, elongated oval, scarlet, very rich in vitamin C and long used as the basis of rose-hip syrup.
SPECIAL FEATURES
Very variable in leaf size, thorniness and general habit.

SHADE TOLERANCE
Moderate to almost deep.
WEATHER TOLERANCE
Good.
PRUNING – I

Rosa canina

Rosa eglanteria

Rosa eglanteria
(syn. *Rosa rubiginosa*) Sweet Brier

" *Another long-familiar native rose; this was Shakespeare's 'sweet eglantine', although it is not as common in Britain as* Rosa canina. *It has a very special merit, however, which has given rise to the epithet 'sweet': the glands on the foliage produce a delicate and sweet perfume. This is especially pronounced when it is growing in a warm and sheltered spot – that bank of Shakespeare's, 'over-canopied with luscious woodbine', would do very nicely. Like the dog rose, this is another good plant for the wild garden or hedgerow and will indeed form a pretty tough and effective barrier on its own, its thorniness helping to make it impenetrable.* "

RELATED ROSES
Lord Penzance's Sweet Briers are a group of hybrids between *Rosa eglanteria* and other roses, bred by the aforementioned gentleman at the end of the nineteenth century. They have inherited some of the foliage fragrance but are generally only of medium height. Among the best of those still available are the pinkish-yellow 'Lord Penzance' (*Rosa eglanteria* x *R.* x *harisonii*, the 'Yellow Rose of Texas') and the rich pink, yellow-centred 'Lady Penzance' (*R. eglanteria* x *R. foetida bicolor*), which has retained the strongest scent of them all.

FORM
Tall, rather lax shrub.
FLOWERS
Single, small, pink, fragrant, summer.
HIPS
Medium, oval, rich red.
SPECIAL FEATURES
Richly fragrant foliage, with a sweet aroma, often said to resemble apples.

SHADE TOLERANCE
Moderate to almost deep.
WEATHER TOLERANCE
Moderate.
PRUNING – I

OTHER RECOMMENDED ROSES
Rosa bracteata 'The McCartney Rose', a medium shrub, single white strangely fragrant flowers with yellow centres, blooms most of the summer, elongated red hips, slightly tender. Best known as one parent of the beautiful climber 'Mermaid' (p.39). China. *Rosa californica plena*, a medium to tall upright shrub, semi-double, pink-lilac, fairly fragrant flowers, summer. Western North America. *Rosa carolina*, a small, compact shrub, single pink fragrant flowers, round red hips. North America. *Rosa caudata*, a medium shrub, single pale pink slightly fragrant flowers, flask-shaped bristly red hips. *R. setipoda* is a similar and perhaps more widely available species. China.

SPECIES AND NEAR-SPECIES

Rosa elegantula persetosa
(syn. *Rosa farreri persetosa*) 'Threepenny Bit Rose'

❝ This is a truly delightful and most interesting shrub. It's a pity that its old botanical name has been superseded, for it commemorated that great plant collector Reginald Farrer from whose seed collection it was raised around 1915 by another great plantsman, E H Bowles. Farrer's Chinese seed was of Rosa elegantula, *a medium-sized shrub with small pale pink flowers and first collected by Ernest Wilson, but among the seedlings raised from it, this one stood out with its better flower colour. The name 'threepenny bit' must puzzle younger gardeners but it is derived from the tiny old silver three pence coin, popularly called a threepenny bit, which was of similar size to the flowers. ❞*

FORM
Medium-sized, rather spreading, arching shrub.

FLOWERS
Single, fairly small, attractive deep pink flowers, summer.

HIPS
Small, broadly spherical, vivid orange-red, very numerous.

SPECIAL FEATURES
Leaves small, fern-like, turning rich red and purple in autumn, masses of rather soft brownish prickles.

SHADE TOLERANCE
Moderate to almost deep.
WEATHER TOLERANCE
Moderate.
PRUNING – 1

Rosa moyesii

Rosa glauca
(syn. *Rosa rubrifolia*)

❝ A beautiful species from mountainous areas of central Europe and yet another rose with a recent change of name. I think that the foliage, which is the main attraction of the plant, can be described as both glaucous and reddish. The leaflets are small, giving an almost fern-like quality and the combination of their form and colour is unique among shrub roses. Nonetheless, the flowers aren't without their beauty and although it is a rather large plant, it is worthy of a place in any mixed border. ❞

FORM
Medium-sized to tall, fairly upright shrub.
FLOWERS
Single, fairly small, purple-pink, slightly fragrant, summer.

HIPS
Small, spherical, red-purple.

SPECIAL FEATURES
Leaves small-medium of a striking greyish purple, good reddish autumn colour, rich purple young stems, rather few prickles.

SHADE TOLERANCE
Moderate.
WEATHER TOLERANCE
Good.
PRUNING – 1

Rosa glauca

RELATED ROSES
The vigorous climber 'Sir Cedric Morris' is a seedling of *Rosa glauca*, almost certainly with *R. mulliganii* as the other parent. It is bigger in all its features, has masses of richly fragrant white flowers and attains a huge size: up to 10m (33ft) tall if grown in good conditions.

Rosa moyesii

66 *In one or other of its selected forms, this must be one of the most popular and best known of all species shrub roses. It was introduced from China in the early years of the twentieth century and, from the beginning, it was impossible to ignore it. Its large, vivid red flowers are unlike those of almost any other rose species and, when taken in combination with its superb fruits, they make a magnificent plant for any garden large enough. But this is a very variable plant, and indeed in the wild, a form with pinker flowers is more common so, before buying, always be sure that your plant has been vegetatively propagated and not raised from seed.* 99

FORM
Medium-sized to tall, fairly spreading shrub.

FLOWERS
Single, rather large, variable from pink to red, but in the best forms, rich blood-red, summer.

HIPS
Medium-sized, elongated flagon-shaped, pendulous, orange-red.

SPECIAL FEATURES
Leaves rather large, dark green.

SHADE TOLERANCE
Moderate to almost deep.
WEATHER TOLERANCE
Good.
PRUNING – 1

RELATED ROSES
Among the several forms and hybrids of this species, I will pick out the two most familiar and, overall, probably the best. 'Geranium' is a seedling selected in the Royal Horticultural Society's garden, England before the Second World War and is the smaller of the two, reaching only medium size and has single flowers described as 'geranium red', which is difficult to interpret; I would describe them as a deep salmon-pink. 'Highdownensis' is a seedling that was found in Sir Frederick Stern's famous chalk garden at Highdown in Sussex, England. It is very vigorous, has rather paler flowers than 'Geranium' but particularly good reddish-coloured hips.

Rosa foetida bicolor
'Austrian Copper'

66 Rosa foetida *is a most important rose species from western Asia, its importance arising from the fact that it has provided one of the main sources of the colour yellow in rose breeding. The double-flowered form 'Persiana' has been used particularly extensively. But this isn't the plant that I grow in my own garden, nor that I recommend here; I prefer the exceptionally striking and unusual flower colours of 'Austrian Copper', an ancient variant, said to have been grown in Arabian gardens before the twelfth century.* 99

FORM
Medium-sized, fairly upright shrub.

FLOWERS
Single, medium-sized, rich copper-red above and vivid yellow beneath, curiously and not very pleasantly fragrant; sometimes a reversion to all-yellow flowers occurs on some branches.

HIPS
Generally absent.

SPECIAL FEATURES
Interesting contrast between brown stems and grey thorns; seriously prone to blackspot.

SHADE TOLERANCE None to light.
WEATHER TOLERANCE
Moderate.
PRUNING – 1

OTHER RECOMMENDED ROSES
Rosa laevigata 'Cherokee Rose', a very tall Chinese shrub or scrambling climber (though naturalized in North America, hence the name), large, single white very fragrant late-spring flowers, ovoid, bristly red fruit. Beautiful but rather tender, needing the shelter of a warm wall. 'Cooperi' ('Cooper's Burmese'), cream flowers and rich dark green leaves. A hybrid derived from this species. *Rosa macrophylla* 'Master Hugh', a superb tall shrub with medium-sized, reddish-pink slightly fragrant flowers but grown for its very large, flagon-shaped orange-red hips; I have never grown a rose with a larger fruit. Nepal.

SPECIES AND NEAR-SPECIES

Rosa pimpinellifolia
'Burnet' or 'Scotch Rose'

66 *The epithet 'ferny' is used to describe the foliage of a number of small-leafed roses but it is never more appropriate than when applied to this species and types derived from it. It is a native British plant but occurs throughout Europe too. It has many merits as a garden plant, not least as a very tough, ground-covering shrub for exposed areas. During the nineteenth century, the varieties derived from this species were legion and among them were numerous doubles but sadly very few survive.* 99

SHADE TOLERANCE None to light.
WEATHER TOLERANCE Moderate.
PRUNING – 1

Rosa pimpinellifolia

FORM
Medium-sized, spreading shrub.
FLOWERS
Single, medium-sized, cream-white, sweetly fragrant, summer.
HIPS
Small, spherical, very dark purple.
SPECIAL FEATURES
Small, very dainty foliage, suckers and spreads freely.

Rosa primula
'Incense Rose'

66 *This is a beautiful plant from Central Asia but I find it slightly tricky and frustrating to grow. It is one of the earliest species to flower in my garden where only the closely related 'Canary Bird' can reliably beat it into bloom. The flowers are a very soft and appealing yellow, but it is the small, fern-like foliage that gives it its common name, as it has an endearing fragrance in hot sun or when crushed. The problem with this rose is persistent tendency for one or two of its shoots to die back each year, something that I know other gardeners have encountered. I suspect that it may be caused by a need for a rather heavier soil than I can provide.* 99

FORM
Medium-sized, fairly upright shrub.
FLOWERS
Single, medium-sized, pale primrose-yellow, very fragrant, spring.
HIPS
I think that small, spherical, red fruit may be formed sometimes although my plant never produces them.
SPECIAL FEATURES
Very pretty, small-leaved and fragrant foliage, very early to flower.

SHADE TOLERANCE None to light.
WEATHER TOLERANCE Moderate.
PRUNING – 1

RELATED ROSES

'Dunwich Rose' is quite lovely and my favourite of the group, and was first found in the 1950s growing wild on the east coast of England with a mass of single, cream-white superbly fragrant flowers, light green foliage and masses of prickles. I grow it through the gravel at the edge of a broad walk where it forms a neat mound, (p.14) although it is invariably rather taller than is usually claimed; I prune mine back to about 1m (3ft). 'Falkland' is a compact shrub with semi-double pale pink flowers that has become very popular although I don't know the origin either of the variety or its name. 'Stanwell Perpetual' (probably *Rosa pimpinellifolia* x *Rosa* x *damascena bifera*) was found in a garden in southern England in 1838 and has double, fragrant soft pink flowers and, as its name suggests, is unique among the group in flowering on and off throughout the summer.

There are many other valuable garden roses that have R. pimpinellifolia somewhere in their ancestry; see for example 'Golden Wings' (p.73), 'Frühlingsgold' (p.72) and 'Maigold' (p.115).

Rosa primula

Rosa sericea omeiensis pteracantha

> *The only reason for growing this Chinese species is that it has probably the largest and certainly the most spectacular thorns that you are ever likely to see. They are red and translucent when young and glow like jewels if the sun shines through them. This is a plant that I recommend whenever I'm asked for suggestions of an anti-social boundary plant to deter intruders but it is certainly worthy of a place in larger gardens for its unique ornamental value too.*

FORM
Tall, rather upright shrub.

FLOWERS
Single, small, white, each with only four petals, slightly fragrant, spring.

HIPS
Small, more or less spherical, orange-red.

SPECIAL FEATURES
Huge thorns on young shoots.

SHADE TOLERANCE
Moderate.
WEATHER TOLERANCE
Moderate.
PRUNING – 1; but prune back up to one-third of the shoots to the base each spring to encourage new growth with the attractive thorns.

RELATED ROSE
'Hidcote Gold' is a very fine plant first grown at Hidcote in the English county of Gloucestershire, shortly after the Second World War and, although of only medium height, it combines thorns almost the size of those of the species with very attractive single yellow flowers. Its origin is not known but it is widely thought to be a cross between *Rosa sericea* and the yellow-flowered *Rosa hugonis*.

OTHER RECOMMENDED ROSES
Rosa nitida, a small suckering shrub, fern-like foliage with good autumn colour, small, single, pink flowers and bristly red fruits. North America. *Rosa nutkana*, a medium-sized, upright shrub, single, lilac-pink, slightly fragrant flowers and small hips. North America. *Rosa x richardii* 'Holy Rose' (although I've also seen it called 'St John's Rose'), a medium-sized spreading shrub, single, pink fragrant flowers and very long persisting hips. This single-flowered rose grows close to my main garden gate. It is probably a natural hybrid between *R. gallica* and *R. phoenicea* (p.12). *Rosa roxburghii* 'Burr Rose', 'Chestnut Rose', a medium-sized, spreading shrub with much-divided leaves, single, pale pink fragrant flowers and orange hips. China. *Rosa souleiana*, a tall, spreading shrub or scrambling climber with yellow thorns, single white flowers and orange-red hips. China.

SPECIES AND NEAR-SPECIES

Rosa xanthina

❝ It was my first impression of China: the drive from Beijing airport to the city, and the road was lined for much of the way with a bright yellow-flowered shrub rose. At a first glance, I thought that it was 'Canary Bird', familiar from my own garden, but when I looked at close quarters, I saw that the plant had the semi-double flowers that revealed it as a 'Canary Bird' parent, the native Chinese species Rosa xanthina. I'm not really sure why it isn't grown more in gardens for it is similarly early, if perhaps rather less tidy. ❞

FORM
Tall, fairly upright but rather loose, angular shrub.

FLOWERS
Semi-double, small to medium-sized, bright yellow, fragrant, spring.

HIPS
Small, more or less spherical, dark red but seeming to drop very soon after they have appeared.

SPECIAL FEATURES
Small-leaved, ferny foliage, flowers very early in the season.

SHADE TOLERANCE Light.
WEATHER TOLERANCE Moderate.
PRUNING – 1

RELATED ROSE

'Canary Bird' (most probably Rosa xanthina x R. hugonis but sometimes called R. xanthina spontanea) – is a much more familiar garden plant, differing from its parent in the larger, single fragrant flowers. It has a fine arching habit that makes it a good, although rather vigorous subject as a weeping standard. Exactly as with R. primula (p.36), some shoots are prone to die back rather mysteriously.

'Canary Bird'

RELATED ROSE

'Rose d'Amour' or 'St Mark's Rose' is almost certainly a hybrid with Rosa virginiana as one parent. It has the same late-flowering characteristic but differs in its taller growth and its charming fully double pink flowers.

SHADE TOLERANCE Moderate.
WEATHER TOLERANCE Moderate.
Pruning – 1

Rosa virginiana

❝ Another of the North American species and one of the most neglected but a useful suckering plant for ground cover in larger gardens. It is useful in a mixed-species planting as it flowers later than most others, combines attractive flowers with good perfume, and has appealing and persistent hips. ❞

FORM
Medium-sized, spreading, bushy and suckering shrub.

FLOWERS
Single, rich pink with striking gold stamens, fragrant, mid- to late summer.

HIPS
Small, vivid red, persistent.

SPECIAL FEATURES
Good yellow and red autumn foliage colours, rather attractive bronze young stems with few thorns.

Rosa virginiana

SPECIES CLIMBERS

Although several of the taller-growing species roses can double up as climbers, or at least benefit from being given the partial support of a tall tripod, there are a few others that are well worth growing as climbers in their own right. But, by and large, they are plants that should be used with caution for some of the most vigorous of all roses are included in this section.

Rosa bracteata
'Mermaid'

❝ I've briefly described the Chinese shrub rose, Rosa bracteata, on p.33. It's a good enough plant but it would never have achieved much recognition had it not been for the English rose breeder William Paul who crossed it with a mystery yellow tea rose to produce, in 1918, one of the most enduringly lovely although frustrating of all climbers in 'Mermaid'. It flowers on and off throughout the summer, has very good disease resistance but isn't reliably hardy. I've tried it time and again in my garden in central England and it won't have it, but give it shelter and warmth and it is a beauty. ❞

'Mermaid'

SHADE TOLERANCE Light to moderate.
WEATHER TOLERANCE Poor.
PRUNING – 7

Rosa filipes 'Kiftsgate'

❝ This plant has one claim to fame: it is the most vigorous climbing rose in captivity. The original specimen, in the garden of Kiftsgate Court, England in which it was first found, is truly gigantic. Its origin isn't known but it is assumed to be a sport of the Chinese species rather than a hybrid. One that I grew through an old apple tree produced shoots 5m (16ft) long in its second year. So if you have a large garden and a large old tree through which it can be grown, then plant 'Kiftsgate'; if not, don't. ❞

FORM
Tall climber.
FLOWERS
Single, fragrant cream-white, in massed clusters; the crown of an old tree filled with the flowers in early summer is an unforgettable sight.
HIPS
Small, broadly spherical, orange-red.
SPECIAL FEATURES
Although its vigour surpasses all other features, it would nonetheless be a very beautiful plant if only it were half the size.

FORM
Tall climber.
FLOWERS
Single, pale yellow moderately fragrant flowers, more or less continuous.
HIPS
None.
SPECIAL FEATURES
No other single-flowered yellow climber blooms for so long. Disease resistant.

OTHER RECOMMENDED ROSES
Rosa brunonii 'La Mortola', a form of a Himalayan species that arose in the gardens of La Mortola in Italy; its main feature is the very greyish foliage which sets off the masses of single white flowers. *Rosa longicuspis*, somewhat similar to *R. filipes* 'Kiftsgate' but rather less vigorous and lacking much of the perfume. Said to be all but evergreen although I haven't found it markedly so. Often confused with *R. mulliganii*. China. *Rosa banksiae lutea*, in the right site, a vigorous and exquisite plant with masses of small, double yellow flowers in summer, not fully hardy and must have a high, warm sheltered wall. China.

SHADE TOLERANCE
Moderate to deep.
WEATHER TOLERANCE
Moderate to good.
Pruning – 7

GALLICAS

The shrub roses known as the Gallicas are ideal for anyone who is interested in old shrub varieties but has limited space, for few will attain more than 1.2m (4ft) in height. Like most other old varieties, they are almost invariably early summer-flowering only and offer a limited range of colours. Most are very fragrant. The true Gallicas are all derived from *Rosa gallica*, a relatively unsophisticated southern and eastern European species with single pink flowers, but the origins of many of the varieties are now obscure. They constitute certainly the oldest and probably largest group of garden roses with some varieties dating from before the seventeenth century although additions have been made over the years and many of those we grow today are nineteenth century plants. The Gallicas have, in turn, contributed to the development of the other major groups of old garden roses and a range of them should be in every rose collection.

Rosa gallica officinalis
'Red Rose of Lancaster', 'Apothecary's Rose'
[Probably pre-thirteenth century]

❝ *Whether or not this is truly the red rose that Edmund Crouchback, Earl of Lancaster, adopted as the emblem of the House of Lancaster in the thirteenth century will never be known. But this is certainly the oldest surviving Gallica variety and appears to be the variety grown extensively in France for use in perfume manufacture, and said to have been brought West originally by returning Crusaders. The name 'Apothecary's Rose' arises because of its extensive medicinal use until recent times; the petals serving as a source of treatments for such disparate conditions as diarrhoea and heavy periods. It would be worthy of a place in the garden on historical grounds alone but it is also a beautiful plant in its own right.* ❞

Rosa gallica officinalis

FORM
Short, fairly upright and compact shrub.

FLOWERS
Semi-double, medium-sized, crimson with gold stamens, fragrant, summer.

HIPS
Small, spherical-oval, red.

SPECIAL FEATURES
Very valuable when grown on its own roots as it suckers readily and thus makes valuable ground cover.

SHADE TOLERANCE Light to moderate.
WEATHER TOLERANCE Moderate.
PRUNING – 1

RELATED ROSE
Rosa gallica versicolor 'Rosa Mundi' [Probably pre-thirteenth century], a very old sport from *R. g. officinalis* and similar in all regards except for its colour: pale pink with stripes and splashes of light crimson with occasional reversions to all red. It has attracted attention for centuries and the name is supposed to commemorate 'Fair Rosamund', the mistress of King Henry II of England, said to have been poisoned by Queen Eleanor.

'Cardinal de Richelieu'
[Around 1840]

❝ *This is the rose that I always quote as the typical Gallica although it is a relatively recent variety. Even among a group with some of the richest and deepest velvety colours of all roses, this one is really dark and will always attract attention for that reason. Its origins are rather obscure and although it is usually said to have been bred in France by the nursery of Jules Laffay, a renowned breeder of Hybrid Perpetuals (p.69), there is some evidence that it is an older Dutch variety.* ❞

FORM
Medium-sized, fairly upright, compact shrub.
FLOWERS
Double, rich purple, darkening as they open and mature, exceptionally fragrant, summer.
HIPS
None.
SPECIAL FEATURES
Almost thornless but with rather spindly stems. There is plenty of smooth, dark green foliage.

SHADE TOLERANCE None to light.
WEATHER TOLERANCE Poor to moderate.
PRUNING – 1, fairly hard.

'Cardinal de Richelieu'

'Complicata' (syn. *Rosa gallica* 'Complicata' or *Rosa macrantha* 'Complicata') [Unknown origin]

❝ *This is an unusual rose in being as close as Gallicas come to climbing. I grow it as a tall shrub in a pyramid but being taller than most it would make a short climber or probably an attractive pillar rose. I'm told on good authority that it is the best of the Gallicas, and one of the best of all old shrub varieties for growing in more free draining and less rich soil.* ❞

FORM
Tall, rather spreading shrub but can be grown as a short climber.
FLOWERS
Single, rather large, mid-pink, much paler in centre and with gold stamens, abundant, very fragrant, summer.

'Complicata'

HIPS
Sparse or none.
SPECIAL FEATURES
Vigorous, could perhaps be used as a tall hedge if not very exposed.

OTHER RECOMMENDED ROSES

'Belle de Crécy' [About 1840], a small to medium-sized shrub, double, rather ragged flowers (I find them a bit messy), pink-mauve, quartered, green eye, very fragrant, summer.

'Charles de Mills' [Unknown origin], small to medium-sized fairly upright but slightly weak-stemmed shrub; very large double, flat, rich-crimson purple, quartered flowers with small green eye, very fragrant, summer.

'Du Maître d'Ecole' [1840], a small, spreading shrub, very large double, deep pink-mauve, flat, quartered flowers with green eye, very fragrant, summer.

SHADE TOLERANCE Light to moderate.
WEATHER TOLERANCE Moderate.
PRUNING – 1

GALLICAS

'Duc de Guiche' [Around 1830, Prevost, France]

Although I generally prefer the rather darker mauve-purple Gallicas, this variety with its more crimson flowers is still a fine plant. It's another of the larger flowered forms and, in my experience, has a more pronounced green eye than any other. If you like this feature, you'll probably find 'Duc de Guiche' to your liking.

'Duc de Guiche'

FORM
Small to medium-sized, rather spreading shrub.

FLOWERS
Double, beautifully formed, large, rich deep violet-crimson coloured, cup-shaped, central green eye, very fragrant, summer.

HIPS
None.

SPECIAL FEATURES
Unusual colouring, tolerant of poorer soils than many other varieties. Attractive dark green foliage.

SHADE TOLERANCE
Moderate.
WEATHER TOLERANCE
Moderate.
Pruning – 1

'Duchesse de Montebello'
[Around 1829, Laffay, France]

This variety has flowers at one extreme of the Gallica form. Many varieties have blooms that open to become almost completely flat, but 'Duchesse de Montebello', like some of the other best pink Gallicas, forms beautiful cup-shaped flowers. Indeed, so extreme are these flowers in their colour and form that there have been suggestions that it isn't truly a Gallica but a cross with a repeat-flowering variety, for plants derived from it may in turn have the repeat-flowering characteristic. But enjoy it, whatever its ancestry, because it is undoubtedly a most splendid rose.

FORM
Small to medium-sized, upright, fairly compact shrub.

FLOWERS
Double, medium-sized, pale soft pink cup-shaped, very fragrant, summer.

HIPS
None.

SPECIAL FEATURES
Unusual combination of colour and shape, fairly tolerant of poorer soils.

SHADE TOLERANCE Light to moderate.
WEATHER TOLERANCE Poor to moderate.
PRUNING – 1

'Duchesse de Montebello'

'Duchesse d'Angoulême' [Around 1825, Vibert, France]

“ *This was the first Gallica that I ever grew and so it has a special place in my affections. In truth, it isn't all that typical of a Gallica, either in its colour or its habit which is a bit weak and floppy, suggesting that something else other than* Rosa gallica *has played a part in its origins;* Rosa centifolia *is usually suggested. Its combination of shell-pink and cup-like shape isn't common, at least on a shrub of this size; with discrete support, this does make a lovely plant.* ”

'Duchesse d'Angoulême'

FORM
Small to medium-sized, upright, rather loose, arching shrub.

FLOWERS
Double, medium-sized, pale soft pink cup-shaped, very fragrant, summer.

HIPS
None.

SPECIAL FEATURES
Unusual combination of both colour and shape, fairly tolerant of poorer soils. Benefits from some careful support, particularly when grown in an exposed position.

SHADE TOLERANCE None to light.
WEATHER TOLERANCE Poor to moderate.
PRUNING – I

'Hippolyte'

'Tuscany Superb' [Around 1848, Paul, England]

“ *For reasons that I can never quite define, this has remained my favourite Gallica over the years. It may have something to do with where I grow it, for it is in my herb garden, close to some lavender and in front of the lush green foliage of fennel which seems to set off the deep mauve flowers perfectly. It's also one of the less 'advanced' Gallicas, not differing vastly from the species. It is, in fact, a sport from an older variety called 'Old Velvet Rose' or 'Tuscany' but with all of its characteristics slightly but 'superbly' exaggerated.* ”

FORM
Small to medium-sized, upright, but somewhat arching shrub.

FLOWERS
Semi-double, medium-sized flowers, beautiful rich dark velvety red with pronounced gold stamens, very fragrant, summer.

HIPS
Sparse.

SPECIAL FEATURES
A magnificent dark colour but be warned that it tends to grow somewhat taller than many nurseries indicate. Few thorns on the strong stems. Good for growing in a small space.

OTHER RECOMMENDED ROSES
'Georges Vibert' [1853, Robert, France], a small to medium upright and thorny shrub, small double pink flowers with crimson stripes, narrow petals, fragrant, summer.
'Hippolyte' [Around 1820], a medium-sized to tall, fairly thornless and lush-foliaged shrub, small double, deep red-purple, at first flattish flowers, fairly fragrant, summer.

SHADE TOLERANCE Light to moderate.
WEATHER TOLERANCE Good to moderate.
PRUNING – I

CENTIFOLIAS

This lovely group of roses has masqueraded under a number of names including **Provence Roses** (pretty inappropriate because they certainly didn't originate there), **Cabbage Roses** (pretty unflattering, although the form of the flowers does bear a passing resemblance to a small and very beautiful cabbage), and **Centifolias** (literally 'one hundred leaves', although if you read petals for leaves, you might be nearer the mark). They are a delicious assemblage of rather thorny, generally medium-sized and very fragrant shrubs and include my favourite of all roses.

For such a familiar and popular group their origins have been long disputed. They were once thought to be the most ancient of roses but it is now reckoned that they originated in Holland from a plant called *Rosa x centifolia* although this rose was not a true species but a complex hybrid. This complicated background might be the reason why the Centifolias are so prone to produce sports and one very distinct group, the **Moss Roses** (p.46), is derived from them.

'Petite de Hollande'

'Blanchefleur'
[1835, Vibert, France]

" An exquisite, uniquely almost white Centifolia but with an exaggerated tendency to bow its flower heads, so full of petals and heavy are they. It has also inherited that rather lax, spreading habit that makes it less than suitable in smaller gardens. But if you want a white Centifolia, there's really nothing else. "

FORM
Medium-sized, rather spreading shrub.

FLOWERS
Double, white with slight touches of pink, cup-shaped, very fragrant, summer.

HIPS
None.

SPECIAL FEATURES
Very thorny with rather distinctive, soft, pale green foliage.

SHADE TOLERANCE Light to moderate.
WEATHER TOLERANCE Poor to moderate.
PRUNING – I

Rosa x centifolia 'Cabbage Rose' or 'Provence Rose' [Unknown origin, pre-seventeenth century]

" This is probably the rose from which the other Centifolias were derived and it certainly seems a synthesis of the features that characterize the group. At its best, it is a truly beautiful shrub although I've never grown it for the single reason that it can look a pretty sad mess in poor summers. My feeling is that it should be kept for warmer, drier gardens where it will be seen at its best, and that where conditions are less reliable, one of the other members of the group should be chosen instead. "

FORM
Medium-sized, rather spreading shrub.

FLOWERS
Double, slightly incurved ('cabbage-like'), medium-sized, rich shell-pink, very fragrant, summer.

HIPS
None.

SPECIAL FEATURES
Beautiful fragrance but a drawback is that the flowers can droop rather unappealingly. Like several of the varieties derived from it, it is prone to mildew.

SHADE TOLERANCE Light to moderate.
WEATHER TOLERANCE Poor.
PRUNING – I

RELATED ROSE
Rosa x centifolia 'Bullata' [Pre-seventeenth century] is sometimes called the lettuce-leaved rose (a real vegetable group this one), for its leaves are abnormally large and wavy, somewhat fancifully like those of a lettuce. Otherwise it is identical to *Rosa x centifolia*. (See also *Rosa x centifolia* 'Cristata' and *Rosa x centifolia* 'Muscosa' p.46.)

'Fantin-Latour' [Unknown origin]

Inevitably, I am often asked for the name of my favourite rose and while this must be one of the hardest questions in gardening, if pressed, this variety is my answer. It seems to sum up so much of what I love about roses and it even has the added appeal of mysterious origins. Although it has the flowers of a Centifolia, it has the leaves of a China rose while some rose experts say that its perfume is that of an Alba. It was named after the nineteenth-century French painter, Henri Fantin-Latour, but that is about all that I can tell you. If you want to know more, then you will simply have to grow it.

FORM

Medium-sized, fairly upright shrub.

FLOWERS

Double, shell pink, cup-shaped, very fragrant, summer.

HIPS

None.

SPECIAL FEATURES

I find it has rather a neater habit than many Centifolias; testimony perhaps to its mixed ancestry, or to my bias.

SHADE TOLERANCE Light to moderate.
WEATHER TOLERANCE Moderate.
PRUNING – 1

'Fantin-Latour'

'De Meaux' (syn. 'Rose de Meaux') [Around 1789, Sweet, England]

Many people maintain that all old shrub roses are just too big for small modern gardens. Some undeniably are too large but this rose and the two that I have recommended are good exceptions and make fine plants for growing in a limited space. As with many of the French names of roses, I have no idea what 'De Meaux' means but it is, in any event, generally reckoned to be an English variety and its origin is usually attributed in some fairly vague manner to the botanist Robert Sweet, who also played some, equally vague, part in the origin of the genuine Miniature Roses (p.80).

FORM

Small, rather compact shrub.

FLOWERS

Double, rich pink, cup-shaped, fairly fragrant, summer.

HIPS

None.

SPECIAL FEATURES

Neat, compact form but like almost all small roses, it must have good growing conditions to be really successful.

SHADE TOLERANCE None to light.
WEATHER TOLERANCE Moderate.
PRUNING – 1, fairly light.

'De Meaux'

OTHER RECOMMENDED ROSES

'Spong' [1805, variously described as French or English and bred by a man named Spong], a small shrub, double, rich pink flowers, very fragrant, summer, intolerant of poor conditions or wet weather. 'Petite de Hollande' [Around 1800, Holland], a small shrub, double, rich pink flowers, fragrant, summer, intolerant of poor conditions.

MOSS ROSES

The natural arising of genetic freaks has played a major part in the development of garden plants, and roses have had their fair share. When the freak takes the form of flowers of a different colour or a compact habit, it is welcomed but generally considered unremarkable. The mutation in the Centifolias that produced the Moss Roses, however, was rather more odd. The pimple-like glands that are present on the sepals are elongated and hair-like, giving the appearance on the flower buds and sometimes other parts of being covered with a mossy-like growth. No-one knows when the mutation occurred, but it was over 300 years ago. You either like them or you don't. I do and grow several, including one of the few Miniature Moss Roses (see p.82).

'Shailer's White Moss'

Rosa x *centifolia* 'Muscosa' [Seventeenth century]

This is a mossed form of Rosa centifolia *and similar to it in all other respects. It is one of the more extensively mossed varieties with the growth taking the form of red-brown bristles on sepals and upper parts of the young shoots.*

FORM
Medium-sized, rather spreading shrub.
FLOWERS
Double, slightly incurved, medium-sized, shell-pink, very fragrant, summer.

HIPS
None.
SPECIAL FEATURES
Fine fragrance, but I find that the flowers of this variety droop unattractively. Very prone to mildew.

SHADE TOLERANCE None to light.
WEATHER TOLERANCE Poor.
PRUNING – 1

RELATED ROSES
Rosa x *centifolia* 'Cristata' [1826, Vibert, France] (syn. 'Cristata', 'Crested Moss', 'Chapeau de Napoléan'), very similar to *Rosa* x *centifolia* 'Muscosa' but the effect is more emphatic than mere mossing and takes the form of rather fleshy outgrowths of the sepals. I confess to finding this a bit extreme and prefer the 'proper' moss.
'Shailer's White Moss' [1788, Shailer, England] (syn. *Rosa centifolia* x *muscosa alba*, 'Clifton Rose', 'White Bath') is supposed to be a white sport either of *Rosa* x *centifolia* 'Muscosa' or another mossed sport of *Rosa* x *centifolia* called 'Common Moss' or 'Old Pink Moss'. Either way, it is a medium-sized, rather spreading shrub and certainly the best white moss with double white summer flowers, tinged with pink, flat and quartered, a strong fragrance but the usual susceptibility to mildew.

'Cristata'

'Alfred de Dalmas'
(syn. 'Mousseline') [1855, Portemer, France]

❝ This was the first Moss Rose I planted in my present garden and it remains one of my favourites, particularly for its long flowering season, which is most unusual in the group. The drawback is that there are few flowers at any one time and the mossed effect is rather sparse – but you can't have everything. Its rather different characteristics are explained by the fact that it isn't derived from the Centifolias but almost certainly from one of the Portland group of the Damasks (p.49). ❞

FORM
Small, rather upright shrub.

FLOWERS
Semi-double, pale pink, cup-shaped, moderately fragrant, repeat-flowering.

HIPS
None.

SPECIAL FEATURES
Neat growth, thrives well in poor soils.

SHADE TOLERANCE Moderate.
WEATHER TOLERANCE Moderate.
PRUNING – I

'William Lobb' (syn. 'Old Velvet Moss', 'Old Velvet Rose', 'Duchesse d'Istrie') [1855, Laffay, France]

❝ This is a very impressive plant, one of the Frenchman Jules Laffay's great triumphs, although I'm unsure whether he bred it or just found it. It is probably the closest we have to a climbing Moss and although I've never tried it, I rather suspect it would make a very good pillar rose. ❞

FORM
Tall, fairly spreading shrub.

FLOWERS
Double, large, purplish-pink with grey overtones, very fragrant, summer.

HIPS
None.

SPECIAL FEATURES
Unusual and striking blooms borne in large numbers in massed heads.

'William Lobb'

SHADE TOLERANCE None to light.
WEATHER TOLERANCE Moderate.
PRUNING – I

'Gloire des Mousseux'
[1852, Laffay, France]

❝ This is most appropriately named, for no Moss Rose has larger or more sumptuous flowers. It is an impressive plant provided you can give it impressive weather, for those very full flowers are prone to damage. The best one I ever saw was in a warm sheltered corner between two walls with a little cover provided by a redundant porch. The growth and perfume were quite remarkable. ❞

FORM
Medium-sized, rather upright shrub.

FLOWERS
Double, very large, shell-pink, very fragrant, summer.

HIPS
None.

SPECIAL FEATURES
A manageable size for a shrub with such large flowers, green mossing.

SHADE TOLERANCE None to light.
WEATHER TOLERANCE Poor.
PRUNING – I

OTHER RECOMMENDED ROSE
'Capitaine John Ingram' [Around 1855, Laffay, France], a small, upright and compact shrub, medium-sized dark purple flowers with rather pronounced eye, very fragrant, rather sparse but attractive reddish moss, summer.

DAMASKS

Why the name Damask and what is its connection, if any, with the cloth of the same name? The connection is Damascus, where the cloth was made originally and whence apparently came a plant called *Rosa damascena*, or, since it is clearly a hybrid, *Rosa x damascena*. Many things that were probably brought back by the Crusaders were credited as coming from Damascus. Nonetheless, the Damasks are clearly an old group. Most are pink, most have the characteristic heavy perfume that was much used in perfumery, most are thorny and medium-sized to fairly tall, so are perhaps less useful in modern gardens.

Rosa x damascena semperflorens
'Quatre Saisons' (syn. *Rosa x damascena bifera*, 'Autumn Damask') [Unknown origin but very old, possibly *Rosa gallica x Rosa moschata*]

" *Most of the names associated with this most important rose bear some reference to its outstanding characteristic: that of repeat-flowering and bearing blooms until well into the autumn. It must have had a remarkable impact when first brought to the West, for no other rose with this characteristic was known until the Chinas were introduced at the end of the eighteenth century and it has remained a rose of great virtue, both for its historic importance and its undeniable beauty. It is also, interestingly, one of the smallest roses of the group.* "

FORM
Medium-sized, rather spreading shrub.

FLOWERS
Loosely double, medium-sized, rather shaggy, pink, very fragrant, repeating.

HIPS
None.

SPECIAL FEATURES
A distinctly leafy rose with much romantic charm. Prone to mildew.

SHADE TOLERANCE None to light.
WEATHER TOLERANCE Moderate.
PRUNING –1

Rosa x damascena versicolor
'York and Lancaster' [Unknown origin but certainly pre-1550]

" *There is a 'Red Rose of Lancaster' and a 'White Rose of York' so it is perhaps fitting that there should be a variety combining both colours. It isn't, of course, a hybrid between them and its flowers are variable. It is untidy but worth having if there is room as it is an old variety even though its historical significance is fanciful.* "

FORM
Medium-sized, rather spreading shrub.

FLOWERS
Semi-double, medium-sized, variable, sometimes pink with some white petals, sometimes white with some pink petals, very fragrant, summer.

HIPS
None.

SPECIAL FEATURES
A curiosity more than a garden plant of real merit.

SHADE TOLERANCE
Moderate.
WEATHER TOLERANCE
Moderate.
PRUNING – 1

Rosa x damascena semperflorens 'Quatre Saisons'

'Ispahan' (syn. 'Rose d'Isfahan', 'Pompon des Princes') [Unknown origin but certainly from the Middle East and pre-1832]

❝ A romantic name for a very beautiful rose, and yet another name that betrays the Middle Eastern origin of the Damasks, Isfahan being the second city of Iran and the ancient capital of Persia. If it wasn't for the towering beauty of 'Madame Hardy' (see below), this definitely would be my favourite of the group as its perfume, even among such company, is probably unmatched. ❞

SHADE TOLERANCE Light.
WEATHER TOLERANCE
Moderate.
PRUNING – 1

'Ispahan'

FORM
Medium-sized, spreading but tidy shrub.
FLOWERS
Double, medium-sized, shell-pink, very fragrant, summer.
HIPS
None.
SPECIAL FEATURES
Rather smaller and less thorny than most Damasks and a wonderful plant.

OTHER RECOMMENDED ROSES

'Celsiana' [Unknown origin but pre-1750], a medium-sized, rather compact shrub, semi-double, rather large pink flowers with gold stamens, very fragrant, summer. 'La Ville de Bruxelles' [1849, Vibert, France], a small to medium-sized upright shrub, although sadly prone to mildew in hot summers, double, quartered, rich pink flowers, very fragrant, summer. 'De Rescht' (syn. 'Rose de Rescht') [Unknown origin], a small, compact shrub, not a true Damask despite the characteristic short flower stalk, but usually grouped with the Portlands which are, in part, descended from them; double, small, rich rose-red flowers in clusters, very fragrant, repeat-flowering. 'Marquesa Boccella' (syn. 'Jacques Cartier') [1868, Moreau-Robert, France] another Portland, a small, compact shrub, double, quartered pink flowers, strong fragrance, more or less continuous-flowering, good shade tolerance.

'Madame Hardy' [1832, Hardy, France]

❝ There is something truly magical about 'Madame Hardy' and there can be few rose growers who wouldn't list it among their top half-dozen old varieties. Monsieur Hardy, who bred the variety and named it after his wife, was a distinguished gardener and rose grower, curator of the Luxembourg Gardens in Paris and apparently sometime gardener to the Empress Josephine. The parentage of his rose is not known but it betrays more than simply Damask in its origin. Ultimately it really doesn't matter as the beauty of this rose transcends mere genetics. ❞

FORM
Medium to tall, spreading but tidy shrub.
FLOWERS
Double, medium, white, with pronounced green eye, fragrant, summer.
HIPS
None.
SPECIAL FEATURES
A very neat plant for one so large, with particularly fresh-looking leaves that perfectly set off the exquisite blooms.

SHADE TOLERANCE
Moderate.
WEATHER TOLERANCE
Moderate.
PRUNING – 1

ALBAS

You don't need to be a classical scholar to deduce that the roses in the group called the Albas should be white. Sadly, you would be wrong as some of the best are pink and I've never been quite sure why the name came to be applied to them all. What is certain is that, like Gallicas and Damasks, they have been with us for a long time. The ancestral type is usually referred to as *Rosa* x *alba* and it is now generally thought to be the result of a cross between a Damask and the native dog rose, *Rosa canina*. The Albas are distinctive and generally rather tall shrubs, supposedly with good disease resistance, although I confess that I have never found them conspicuously better than other groups in this respect. They do, nonetheless, tend to have good shade tolerance and are valuable as single specimens, in groups towards the back of shrub borders or as hedging.

Rosa x *alba* 'White Rose of York'
(syn. *Rosa* x *alba semi-plena*)
[Pre-sixteenth century]

" I've already introduced you to the 'Red Rose of Lancaster' (p.40) and the pink and white 'York and Lancaster' (p.48). This is the third of the historical trio although, as with the others, there is very little or no evidence to associate this variety specifically with the fifteenth-century Richard, Duke of York; but it's a good story. It's not a bad rose either, although perhaps a bit unsophisticated for modern tastes which may be the reason why it has become something of a garden rarity. It's worth adding that you may see the name semi-plena *applied to a different variety but it is now generally reckoned that they are both one and the same. "*

FORM
Medium-sized to tall, fairly upright shrub.

FLOWERS
Single (or almost, the alternative name *semi-plena* implies something bigger but it's more single than not), large, pure white with gold stamens, very fragrant, summer.

HIPS
Medium-sized, elongated oval, scarlet.

SPECIAL FEATURES
This is a big plant and needs a big garden but it is valuable in a large planting, apart from anything else, for its particularly attractive hips.

SHADE TOLERANCE Moderate to almost deep.
WEATHER TOLERANCE Moderate to good.
PRUNING – 1

RELATED ROSE
'Alba Maxima' (syn. 'Jacobite Rose', 'Maxima', 'Great Double White', 'Cheshire Rose', 'Bonnie Prince Charlie's Rose') [Pre-fifteenth century], a tall, upright shrub with double, pale pink summer flowers that open pure white, very fragrant. A very old rose that is often found in old gardens, having failed either to revert or die back but stayed true to type. It has nothing whatever to do with the rebellion of 1745.

'Céleste'
(syn. 'Celestial')
[Unknown origin]

" This is a good name for a very good rose, one of those varieties that belies the name Alba. It's slightly smaller than most in the group, and as far as many gardeners are concerned, all the better for that. My plant is particularly floriferous and seems to have a distinctive perfume that makes me wonder about its ancestry. "

FORM
Medium-sized, fairly upright shrub.

FLOWERS
Semi-double, pink with yellow stamens, very fragrant, summer.

HIPS
None.

SPECIAL FEATURES
This is a rather special variety but with nothing so special that you can put your finger on it, although the combination of both size and vigour are important.

SHADE TOLERANCE Moderate.
WEATHER TOLERANCE Moderate to good.
PRUNING – 1

'Céleste'

'Königin von Danemark' (syn. various other spellings, also 'Queen of Denmark') [1826, Booth, England]

❝ *Two of my rose-growing friends rate this variety the best of all old roses and it's not difficult to see the reasons why, for its flowers have a sublime perfection of form that is hard to surpass. When combined with the sweet fragrance, a fairly restrained growth and the general ease of cultivation that is characteristic of the Albas, the argument becomes jolly compelling.* ❞

FORM
Medium-sized, fairly upright shrub.
FLOWERS
Double, pink, quartered, flat with central 'button', very fragrant, summer.

HIPS
None.
SPECIAL FEATURES
The quartered flowers come as close as those of any of the old rose varieties to resembling crushed tissue-paper.

SHADE TOLERANCE
Moderate.
WEATHER TOLERANCE
Moderate to good.
PRUNING – 1

OTHER RECOMMENDED ROSES
'Félicité Parmentier' [Unknown origin but before about 1830], a medium-sized rather compact shrub, double, quartered, summer flowers, pink, fading to almost white, very fragrant, one of those Albas that really does have reliably good disease resistance.
'Great Maiden's Blush' (syn. 'Maiden's Blush, 'Great', 'Incarnata', 'La Royale', 'La Virginale', 'La Séduisante', 'Cuisse de Nymphe', 'Cuisse de Nymphe Emue', at least some of which were banned by the Victorians; use your French dictionary to find out why) [Pre-sixteenth century], a medium-sized to tall, spreading, arching shrub, flowers double, rather loose, pale pink, very fragrant, summer.
'Maiden's Blush' [1797, Kew Gardens, England] is a scaled-down version of the previous variety from which it may be a sport.

'Königin von Danemark'

RUGOSAS

The Rugosa roses have become so integral and important a part of the shrub rose scene in gardens that it is surprising to realize how recently they arrived. I've seen many a book describe them as being among 'the old shrub roses' which is stretching things a little. Admittedly, the parental plant, *Rosa rugosa*, was introduced from Japan in 1796 and a few of the varieties we grow today date from the nineteenth century but the most popular and best known are twentieth-century hybrids. The plant does, however, have a long history of cultivation in the Far East and may have been growing in Chinese gardens as long as a thousand years ago. Its most remarkable feature, and the one that gives rise to its name, is the very atypical foliage which is rough and bristly or "rugose". The Rugosas, parent and offspring, are very easy to grow, almost pest- and disease-free and incredibly tough.

Rosa rugosa 'Japanese Rose' [1796, Japan]

66 *This rose is rather unusual in being one that has given rise to a large group of hybrids (it seems to be a very promiscuous plant) and yet is still fairly widely grown in its species form. It is a variable plant nonetheless, especially when raised from seed, and you would be advised to select a colour form that particularly appeals to you and propagate it by cuttings.* 99

Rosa rugosa

FORM
Medium-sized to tall shrub, spreading upright habit.
FLOWERS
Single, variable from rather dark red to pale pink with yellow stamens, moderately to very fragrant, more or less continuous.
HIPS
Large to very large, spherical, orange-red.
SPECIAL FEATURES
If you want a really tough rose for an exposed position, even one to create a hedge, then *Rosa rugosa* will probably do it for you better than anything else.

SHADE TOLERANCE
Moderate to almost deep.
WEATHER TOLERANCE
Good.
PRUNING – 1

RELATED ROSE
Rosa rugosa 'Alba' – the white-flowered form of the species, otherwise more or less identical.

'Blanche Double de Coubert'
(*Rosa rugosa* x 'Sombreuil') [1892, Cochet-Cochet, France]

66 *One of the most widely grown white shrub roses and one to which I owe a particular debt, for it was through growing it that I was introduced to one of its parents, the fabulous 'Sombreuil' (p.67). It is a very good rose in all respects bar one: I have yet to see a plant on which the white petals didn't develop a premature brown staining, whatever the weather. Nonetheless if you want a white Rugosa, with all the positive attributes that this brings, you have little choice.* 99

FORM
Medium-sized to tall, spreading shrub.
FLOWERS
Double, white, moderately to very fragrant, repeat-flowering.
HIPS
Rather sparse in most years (my plant hardly ever sets them), large, spherical, orange-red.
SPECIAL FEATURES
The best double white Rugosa, despite its slight floral drawback. But of course, highly disease resistant. Provides good colour in the autumn.

SHADE TOLERANCE
Moderate to almost deep.
WEATHER TOLERANCE
Moderate.
PRUNING – 1

'Blanche Double de Coubert'

'F J Grootendoorst' (*Rosa rugosa* 'Rubra' x 'Madame Norbert Levasseur') [1918, de Goey, Holland]

❝ This is a very distinctive rose, one of the small group of Rugosa hybrids with frill-shaped petals, although not all obtained this characteristic in the same way; this one being a cross with a Polyantha Pompon. It produces a mass of rather small blooms but, in most years, retains at least some flowers for longer into the autumn than any other rose that I grow in my garden. ❞

FORM
Medium-sized to tall, rather upright shrub.
FLOWERS
Double, rather small, crimson with frilled edges to the petals, slightly fragrant (at least on my plants, but I have seen it described as fragrant), continuous-flowering.

'F J Grootendoorst'

HIPS
None.
SPECIAL FEATURES
Not a beautiful rose but with a certain charm although the colour is a bit sickly. Good disease resistance.

RUGOSAS

'Fru Dagmar Hastrup'
(syn. Fru Dagmar Hartopp, Frau Dagmar Hastrup, Frau Dagmar Hartopp) (probably a *Rosa rugosa* seedling) [1914, Hastrup, Denmark]

'Fru Dagmar Hastrup'

❝ *This is probably the most familiar and popular of all of the Rugosas and is many gardeners' introduction to shrub rose growing, for it is of a size that works even in modestly sized gardens. It is also, like its parent, used extensively along the side of roads and in other inhospitable places. By no means are its flowers spectacular although they do repay close inspection for the delicacy of the petals. Close inspection will also reveal the perfume and then, if you keep looking until the autumn, you will see some of the finest hips of any rose.* ❞

FORM
Small, spreading but still neat shrub.

FLOWERS
Single, pale silver-pink, cream stamens, moderately fragrant, repeat- or almost continuous-flowering.

HIPS
Abundant, large, spherical, orange-red.

SPECIAL FEATURES
Virtually trouble-free, a tough, robust but none too large shrub. Very disease and pest resistant.

SHADE TOLERANCE
Moderate.
WEATHER TOLERANCE
Moderate.
PRUNING – I

'Roseraie de l'Haÿ' (Unknown parentage)
[1901, Cochet-Cochet, France]

❝ *The Roseraie de l'Haÿ near Paris is one of the great rose gardens of the world and so it needs a jolly fine rose to bear its name. This is it, one of the most popular and beautiful of all the Rugosa hybrids and one that featured among my own first plantings of roses belonging to this group. The flowers are almost double, borne in rich profusion, of fine colour and fragrance and the plant is of neat if rather tall habit. If there is a drawback, it must be the paucity of hips.* ❞

FORM
Medium-sized to tall, generally neat although spreading shrub.

FLOWERS
Semi-double, rich dark red-purple, cream stamens, very fragrant, repeat- or almost continuous-flowering.

HIPS
Sparse, spherical, orange-red.

SPECIAL FEATURES
The usual Rugosa disease and pest resistance. Another attraction of this rose is that it more often than not produces good yellow foliage colour in the autumn.

'Roseraie de l'Haÿ'

SHADE TOLERANCE
Moderate.
WEATHER TOLERANCE
Moderate.
PRUNING – I

'Sarah van Fleet' (Possibly *Rosa rugosa* x 'My Maryland') [1926, van Fleet, USA]

❝ One of a very small group of North American Rugosa varieties to have achieved popularity in Europe is this – a variety about which I have never been entirely sure. It is beautiful, fragrant, weather resistant but rather on the tall side, thorny and, unusually for a Rugosa, a bit disease-prone. This tendency is presumably acquired through its other parent, which is usually said to be the old pink Hybrid Tea, 'My Maryland', although on the few occasions that I have seen that variety, it has been a dwarf bush, which doesn't seem right as a parent for this plant. ❞

FORM
Medium-sized to tall, upright, dense shrub.
FLOWERS
Semi-double, rich, pink, yellow-gold stamens, very fragrant, repeat-flowering.
HIPS
Rarely seen.
SPECIAL FEATURES
Very thorny, less disease resistant than many in the group and sometimes prone to rust in wet seasons.

SHADE TOLERANCE Moderate.
WEATHER TOLERANCE Moderate.
PRUNING – 1

'Sarah van Fleet'

'Scabrosa'
(Unknown parentage) [1960, Harkness, England]

❝ This is a relatively recent introduction to the Rugosa family that has quickly become popular and it would certainly deserve pride of place in a planting of rose fruits. It is a seedling of Rosa rugosa, *but whether it is just a variant or* actually a hybrid, with something closely related as the other parent, is not known. The foliage is very good and the typical Rugosa coarseness is counter-balanced by a glossy green lushness and veining that many others lack. ❞*

FORM
Medium-sized, upright, dense shrub.
FLOWERS
Abundant, single, large, deep rose-pink blooms, cream-yellow stamens and prominant anthers, moderately fragrant, repeat-flowering.
HIPS
Very large, more or less spherical, orange-red.

SPECIAL FEATURES
Very floriferous, plants seem variable in quality; those from some nurseries taller and more vigorous than others.

SHADE TOLERANCE Moderate.
WEATHER TOLERANCE Moderate.
PRUNING – 1

'Scabrosa'

OTHER RECOMMENDED ROSE
'Schneezwerg' (syn. 'Snow Dwarf') (origin uncertain but possibly *Rosa rugosa* x a Polyantha) [1912, Lambert, Germany], small to medium-sized, neat, compact but spreading shrub, semi-double, white flowers with cream-yellow stamens, very fragrant, small, spherical orange-red hips, continuous-flowering.

HYBRID MUSKS

Just as many people who know little of roses have heard of the Damasks, so they have also heard of the Musk Roses, a name that is redolent of balmy evenings, heavy with sweet and exotic fragrances exuding from sumptuous flowers of ancient origin. How sad, therefore, that the truth should be rather different. Although *Rosa moschata*, the Musk Rose itself, is a species that has been cultivated for centuries, it isn't particularly well scented and the group of varieties known as the Hybrid Musks have only a tenuous ancestral connection with it and are very much twentieth-century plants. This is not to diminish their appeal and in some cases, their very real beauty; it's simply that they aren't what you might have expected.

The connection with the Musk Rose comes through a rather small group of roses called the Noisettes with *Rosa moschata* in their parentage (p.66) and there is an interesting story attached to it. In the very early years of the twentieth century, the German rose breeder Lambert raised a plant called 'Trier', a short climber with masses of small white flowers. It was a seedling of a climbing Polyantha variety called 'Aglaia' which was itself a cross between *Rosa multiflora* and a Noisette called 'Rêve d'Or'. The story then moves to Essex, southern England and to the Reverend Joseph Pemberton and his gardener J A Bentall, who used 'Trier', as well as other Noisette and Polyantha varieties in crosses with Tea and Hybrid Tea Roses to produce the present group, the Hybrid Musks. They are small to medium-sized, fairly spreading but nonetheless neat shrubs with very pretty, simple flowers, many of which still betray in their perfume that ancient musk connection.

'Prosperity'
('Marie-Jeanne' x 'Perle des Jardins') [1919, Pemberton, England]

❝ *This is an interesting and beautiful rose. It was bred by Pemberton and is a cross between a Polyantha and a Tea Rose. Its popularity seems to increase as the years go by. Fortunately, the Tea in its parentage has not served to lessen its hardiness although it does confer the fragrance. It is a particularly floriferous rose with flower heads that are sometimes too heavy for their own good as they have a tendency to bow earthwards.* ❞

'Prosperity'

FORM
Small to medium-sized, upright shrub.

FLOWERS
Double, fairly small but in large clusters, cream-white with pink and yellow flushes, moderately fragrant, summer.

HIPS
None.

SPECIAL FEATURES
Flowering shoots that spread outwards add to its appeal, but mean that it must be given room to display itself.

SHADE TOLERANCE
Light.
WEATHER TOLERANCE
Moderate to poor.
PRUNING – I

'Buff Beauty'
('William Allen Richardson' x unknown rose) [1939, Bentall, England]

❝ 'Buff Beauty' is a ravishing rose with a colour that is among my real favourites, a shade of peach that it shares with 'Gloire de Dijon', 'Perle d'Or' and 'Lady Hillingdon' among other roses that I grow in my garden. It would be fascinating to know where this colour originated. The known parent, 'William Allen Richardson' is a nineteenth-century Noisette of similar hue, and a sport from 'Rêve d'Or', itself a seedling of an even older rose called 'Madame Schultz' but unfortunately this is where the trail goes cold. ❞

FORM
Medium-sized, spreading shrub.

FLOWERS
Double, medium-sized but in large clusters, yellow-peach, moderately fragrant, repeat- to continuous-flowering.

HIPS
None.

SPECIAL FEATURES
A rather unpredictable plant in the variability of the colour intensity from place to place and, to some extent, from season to season, features shared with other roses of this colour.

SHADE TOLERANCE Light.
WEATHER TOLERANCE Moderate to poor.
PRUNING – I

'Francesca' ('Danaë' x 'Sunburst') [1920s, Pemberton, England]

❝ This is one of those roses that I acquired by accident, for it was sent to me by a nursery as a substitute for something else out of stock. I can't remember my original order but I don't much care, for this is truly a rich addition to my collection. And, in truth, it must have been a curious choice as a substitute for there is nothing else quite like it in its colour and form although it can trace a real Hybrid Musk ancestry back to 'Trier' through 'Danaë'. ❞

FORM
Medium-sized to tall, fairly upright shrub.

FLOWERS
Semi-double, medium-sized, apricot-yellow, gradually turning to a more clear yellow, slightly fragrant, repeat- to continuous-flowering.

HIPS
None.

SPECIAL FEATURES
The colour is the significant feature of this rose, falling short of the wonderful yellow-peach of 'Buff Beauty' but, when mature, of a rich yellow shade that is not often seen among shrub roses of any sort.

SHADE TOLERANCE Light to moderate.
WEATHER TOLERANCE Moderate.
PRUNING – I

OTHER RECOMMENDED ROSE
'Moonlight' ('Trier' x 'Sulphurea') [1913, Pemberton, England], a tall, upright shrub, small, semi-double white flowers with yellow stamens, moderately to strongly fragrant, repeat- to continuous-flowering, very vigorous.

'Buff Beauty'

'Moonlight'

HYBRID MUSKS

'Ballerina'
(Unknown parentage) [1937, Bentall, England]

" The most famous, the most popular, the most reliable of all of the Hybrid Musks and arguably Bentall's greatest triumph. It is sad and extraordinary, therefore, that its parentage isn't known but clearly a Polyantha had much to do with it and it is sometimes classified as such. It produces masses of simple, unsophisticated flowers. "

'Ballerina'

FORM
Small to medium-sized, spreading shrub.

FLOWERS
Single, small, in very large clusters, rose-pink with white centres, quite fragrant, repeat- to continuous-flowering.

HIPS
None.

SPECIAL FEATURES
Apart from the huge quantities of flowers, and reliability even in poor soils, the excellent rain-tolerance is itself a singular virtue.

SHADE TOLERANCE Light to moderate.
WEATHER TOLERANCE Very Good.
PRUNING – 1

'Felicia'
('Trier' x 'Ophelia') [1928, Pemberton, England]

" When gardeners learn of my interest in roses, a large number tell me that they grow 'Felicia', which implies that it is one of the 'in' varieties. I'm not sure why it should be singled out for there are better roses and, indeed, several better Hybrid Musks, although it does have a good number of fairly large and finely fragrant flowers. "

FORM
Small to medium-sized, spreading shrub.

HIPS
None.

FLOWERS
Double, fairly large, rather ragged, pink, moderately fragrant, repeat-flowering.

SPECIAL FEATURES
The flowers are larger than usual for a Hybrid Musk and their general form and fragrance owe much to the fact that 'Ophelia', one of the parents, is not a Tea but a Hybrid Tea.

SHADE TOLERANCE Poor.
WEATHER TOLERANCE Moderate to poor.
PRUNING – 1

'Felicia'

CLIMBING HYBRID MUSKS

There is a small group of climbing roses that, although not of the same parentage as the true Hybrid Musks, nonetheless have the Musk Rose somewhere in their ancestry and the best two are included here.

'The Garland' (*Rosa moschata* x *Rosa multiflora*) [1835, Wells, England]

" At its best, 'The Garland' in the height of summer is a fabulous sight with its masses of small flowers, imbuing the air all around with a heady fragrance. But like so many other of the most spectacular climbing roses, it must have room in which to grow, and so is not a plant for small gardens. In some ways it has more in common with ramblers than climbers, including its limited flowering season. "

FORM
Tall climber.
FLOWERS
Semi-double, small, cream-white, rather ragged, very fragrant, summer.
HIPS
Small, red-orange, oval.
SPECIAL FEATURES
There are few climbers that produce so many flowers of this size, for although small, they are individually much larger than those of, say, 'Kiftsgate'.

SHADE TOLERANCE
Moderate.
WEATHER TOLERANCE
Moderate to good.
PRUNING – 7

OTHER RECOMMENDED ROSE
'Paul's Himalayan Musk' (Unknown parentage) [Late nineteenth century, Paul, England] is a tall climber with small, double, unusual lavender-pink slightly fragrant flowers produced on slender stems, small oval orange-red hips, large thorns. Flowers in mid-summer. A fine rose that looks particularly impressive when growing up a large old tree.

'The Garland'

CHINA ROSES

China has played an enormous part in the history of the garden rose and *Rosa chinensis* has played a particularly valuable role. This is because it possesses the capacity for repeat-flowering that differentiates most modern roses from most older ones. Before *Rosa chinensis* reached the West in the mid-eighteenth century, repeat-flowering had been a rare and aberrant characteristic. The Chinese, of course, had known of the value of their native rose for centuries and many varieties were grown in old Chinese gardens. It was thought that the true species no longer existed although, recently, there has been evidence to suggest that a tall shrub with pink flowers known in the wild in the province of Szechuan may indeed be it.

Logically, since all are derived in some way from *Rosa chinensis*, almost any modern rose might be thought eligible to be called a China but I have limited my selection here to a few, rather choice shrubs. These all have the light, open, airy habit that so characterizes the group, and they differ relatively little from *Rosa chinensis* itself. In common with general practice, I have excluded the many, often complex, modern hybrid derivatives which will be found in other sections. But there are no hard and fast rules to this categorization and you will find some writers include varieties such as 'Cécile Brunner' and 'Bloomfield Abundance' which I have grouped with the Polyanthas (p.70).

Rosa x *odorata* 'Mutabilis' (syn. 'Mutabilis', 'Tip Ideale') (Unknown parentage) [1932, from China]

" This rather strange variety is probably an old Chinese garden hybrid although, for a long time it was thought to be a true species and given the name Rosa turkestanica. *It is a lovely thing but I consider it strange as its rather delicate-looking flowers include a whole range of shades of yellow, red and orange while the plant itself varies in height from almost dwarf to rather tall. All of these characteristics suggest a rose with a complex ancestry and my advice is always to buy this variety in person and not by mail-order so that you can see the stock from which it has been raised. "*

SHADE TOLERANCE Light to moderate.
WEATHER TOLERANCE Moderate to good.
PRUNING – 3

FORM
Small to tall, rather upright shrub.

FLOWERS
Single, large, very dainty, opening yellow, then changing through apricot to pink or red, slightly fragrant, repeat- to continuous-flowering.

HIPS
None.

SPECIAL FEATURES
A rose that benefits from some shelter; although it is hardy, it gives a much better account of itself if it is grown in a warmer spot.

Rosa x *odorata* 'Mutabilis'

'Pompon de Paris' (Also a climbing form)
(Unknown parentage) [1839]

❝ I don't think that anyone knows a great deal about the origin of this charming little rose, and its relationship with the Chinas isn't at all clear. What is important, however, is that I like it enormously, both in its bush form and as a most delightful climber. I grow the climbing version over an archway where it intermingles with 'Mrs Herbert Stevens' in a very pretty tangle. It has the merit of flowering very early but its one drawback is that it becomes very twiggy if it is grown in a shaded position. ❞

FORM
Dwarf shrub or medium-sized to tall climber.
FLOWERS
Semi-double ('pompon'-like), tiny, single, rose-pink, no fragrance, more or less confined to summer in climbing form but repeat-flowering as a shrub.
HIPS
None.
SPECIAL FEATURES
Very early-flowering and very floriferous; tends to become rather congested later in the season and dies back at the centre so shoots should be thinned out regularly.

'Pompon de Paris' (climber)

SHADE TOLERANCE None.
WEATHER TOLERANCE
Moderate to good.
PRUNING – 3

'Cramoisi Supérieur' (Also a climbing form)
(Unknown parentage) [1832, Coquereau, France]

❝ A rose to look at rather than to smell for it lacks fragrance but has the most endearing flowers on a very compact shrub. It is a good variety for a collection in a small garden, although I do find its shade of red a trifle difficult to blend with anything else. The climbing form is a useful plant if it can be grown alone, away from other roses, when its distinctive colour may be fully appreciated. ❞

FLOWERS
Semi-double, small, large clusters, cup-shaped, rich, clear, unchanging red, no fragrance, more or less confined to summer in climbing form but repeat-flowering as a shrub.

FORM
Dwarf shrub or medium to tall climber.
HIPS
None.
SPECIAL FEATURES
The climbing form is a good plant for an exposed position in full sun as it holds its colour and doesn't bleach or change under these conditions. Odd petals of the shrub form are sometimes streaked with white. The large flower clusters overcome some of that airy feel that is so often the hallmark of the China roses.

SHADE TOLERANCE Moderate.
WEATHER TOLERANCE
Good.
PRUNING – 1

OTHER RECOMMENDED ROSES
'Champneys' Pink Cluster' (*Rosa chinensis* x *R. moschata*) [1802, Champneys, USA] a tall climber, semi-double to double clear pink, moderately fragrant flowers, vigorous, summer. An interesting plant as it was from this variety that the Noisette group was derived (p.66). 'Gruss an Teplitz' (('Sir Joseph Paxton' x 'Fellemberg') x ('Papa Gontier' x 'Gloire de Rosomanes')) [1897, Geschwind, Hungary], a complex mixture of China, Bourbon and Tea, a tall shrub or medium-sized climber; medium-sized, double, ragged, fragrant, dark red flowers, fading as they mature; rather disease-prone (mildew especially), often recommended for hedging but I find it too lax for the purpose, repeat- to continuous-flowering.

BOURBONS

The Ile de Bourbon is the old name for the stunningly beautiful island of Réunion in the Indian Ocean, not an obvious candidate for a significant role in the history of roses as they don't occur there naturally. They were planted there in the eighteenth century to form boundary hedges, although on a recent visit I was sorry to see that the practice seems to have died out. Among those once grown, however, were the old China rose 'Parson's Pink' (now usually called 'Old Blush') and the Damask 'Quatre Saisons' (p.48). The observant director of the local botanic garden collected seed from a type of rose known locally as 'Rose Edouard' that was found commonly in company with these two, and which was assumed to be their offspring. He sent the seed to France where the variety was used extensively in the development of what became known as the Bourbons. The group includes several very good strong-growing and beautiful shrubs and some fine and famous climbers, all displaying characteristics intermediate between Chinas and Damasks, although generally leaning to one side or the other. The major drawback is that many varieties are unavoidably disease-prone.

'Boule de Neige'
('Blanche Lafitte' x 'Sappho') [1867, Lacharme, France]

An earlier white Bourbon crossed with a cream-coloured Tea Rose produced this, one of the best white-flowered shrub roses and one with the very special virtue, unlike so many others, of not discolouring as it ages. The flowers are only of moderate size and grouped in small heads and when fully open remind me of 'Sombreuil' (p.67), that stunning climbing white Tea Rose. The first time that I ever saw this rose, it was in a demonstration plot and attracted the most attention.

FORM
Medium-sized to tall, upright shrub.

FLOWERS
Double, fairly small but in medium-sized clusters, slightly pink in bud but opening pure white and recurving through flat to form a ball (the "snowball" of the name) with a crumpled centre, very fragrant, repeat-flowering.

HIPS
None.

SPECIAL FEATURES
The purity of the colour and fragrance are superb and with its tall, narrow habit, this is a wonderful rose for a warm sheltered corner of the garden. Attractive glossy foliage.

SHADE TOLERANCE None.
WEATHER TOLERANCE Moderate to poor.
PRUNING – 3

'Boule de Neige'

'Souvenir de la Malmaison' (syn. 'Queen of Beauty and Fragrance') ('Madame Desprez' x an unknown Tea Rose) [1843, Beluze, France]

❝ *This may well be the most widely grown Bourbon shrub but I suspect that this is more because it is named after the Empress Josephine's garden than for its intrinsic merits. Although it does display all the worthy characteristics of the group, and at its best, has fabulous flowers, it isn't always happy in damp summer weather, but give it warmth, dryness and sunshine, and few can match it.* ❞

FORM
Small to fairly tall (a variable variety), spreading shrub (and a climbing form).
FLOWERS
Double, fairly large, salmon-pink, flat flowers, very fragrant, repeat-flowering.
HIPS
None.
SPECIAL FEATURES
A variable plant and really only one for dry parts of the country although even there, it can suffer from mildew.

SHADE TOLERANCE None.
WEATHER TOLERANCE Very poor.
PRUNING – 3

'Souvenir de la Malmaison'

'Variegata di Bologna' (Unknown parentage) [1909, Bonfiglioli, Italy]

❝ *I cannot pretend that I am really a fan of striped roses, but many gardeners obviously are and so I include this one here for their benefit. It has no special merit apart from the striping effect on the petals, although it is interesting in being one of the relatively few popular rose varieties to have been bred in Italy, and also in being, for a Bourbon, fairly late onto the scene.* ❞

FORM
Tall upright shrub (and also available in a climbing form).
FLOWERS
Double, medium-sized, cream-white flowers with red-purple stripes, very fragrant, repeat-flowering.
HIPS
None.

SPECIAL FEATURES
The flower colour of course; mildew- and blackspot-prone.

SHADE TOLERANCE None.
WEATHER TOLERANCE Very poor.
PRUNING – 3

RELATED ROSES
There are two other similar striped Bourbons, 'Commandant Beaurepaire' (Unknown parentage) [1874, Moreau-Robert, France], summer-flowering and with white, pinks, reds and purples in its make-up.
'Honorine de Brabant' (Unknown origin), repeat-flowering and white, pale pink and lilac.

OTHER RECOMMENDED ROSES
'Madame Pierre Oger' (sport from 'La Reine Victoria') [1878, Oger, France], a medium-sized, spreading shrub, double, silver-pink, cupped flowers, very fragrant, very prone to blackspot, repeat-flowering.
'Louise Odier' (Unknown parentage) [1851, Margottin, France] a medium-sized, upright shrub, double, bright rose-pink, rather rounded flowers, very fragrant, less disease-prone than many Bourbons, repeat-flowering.

BOURBONS

'Madame Isaac Pereire'
(Unknown parentage)
[1881, Garcon, France]

" I have grown this rose for some 20 years and I still grow it, in spite of the fact that it has several drawbacks. If I look closely at the flowers on a warm summer's day, I know why it is still in my garden, for if ever a rose personified the word sumptuous, this surely is it. The flowers, held on strong stems, are huge, richly coloured and unkempt in the best traditions of the best shrub roses. Then I stand back and see a rather untidy bush with a generous helping of blackspot and mildew; but then that's life and you can't have everything. "

FORM
Tall, rather spreading shrub.

FLOWERS
Almost double, very large, loose, dark pink-purple with a few yellow stamens, very fragrant, repeat-flowering.

HIPS
None.

SPECIAL FEATURES
The richness of the colour and perfume of the flowers must be offset against the size and relatively unattractive form of the shrub and the susceptibility to blackspot and mildew.

SHADE TOLERANCE Light.
WEATHER TOLERANCE
Moderate.
PRUNING – 3

'Madame Isaac Pereire'

'La Reine Victoria' (Unknown parentage)
[1872, Schwarz, France]

" A variety, that, like its sport 'Madame Pierre Oger', displays the best and the worst of the Bourbons. The flowers are of the luscious pink that invites comment and my experience has been that it flowers more reliably and for longer than any other in the group; but there's also the blackspot. "

FORM
Medium-sized, upright shrub.

FLOWERS
Double, medium-sized, cup-like, lilac-pink, very fragrant, repeat-flowering.

HIPS
None.

SPECIAL FEATURES
Very prone to blackspot and becomes an untidy looking plant when the leaves, in consequence, drop prematurely.

SHADE TOLERANCE None to light.
WEATHER TOLERANCE
Moderate to poor.
PRUNING – 3

OTHER RECOMMENDED ROSE
'Adam Messerich' ('Frau Oberhofgartner Singer' x (a seedling of 'Louise Odier' x 'Louis Phillipe')) [1920, Lambert, Germany] a vigorous, medium-sized, spreading shrub with semi-double, cup-shaped, rich rose-red coloured flowers, fading to a slightly sickly pink as the season progresses, fairly fragrant. More or less repeat-flowering, an interesting, recent Bourbon with Hybrid Tea in its parentage.

CLIMBING BOURBONS

I've already mentioned a few Bourbon shrub varieties that have climbing sports. There are others, of which these are the best, now grown almost exclusively in the climbing form.

'Zéphirine Drouhin' (Unknown parentage)
[1868, Bizot, France]

'La Reine Victoria'

" *One of the most famous of all climbing roses but for one characteristic only. It is almost entirely thornless. Were it not for this, I think that mildew and its relatively undistinguished flowers would have seen it off long ago and, with the advent of newer varieties of modern thornless roses, I wonder how long it will endure. Nonetheless, for the moment, it is a wise choice if you want a climber in a position where people and their clothes are likely to come into contact with it.* "

FORM

Tall climber.

FLOWERS

Semi-double, cerise, or in truth, a sickly pink, very fragrant, repeat-flowering.

HIPS

None.

SPECIAL FEATURES

The almost thornless shoots outweigh all other features except the susceptibility to mildew which is surpassed only by some Ramblers.

SHADE TOLERANCE
Moderate.
WEATHER TOLERANCE
Good.
PRUNING – 2

RELATED ROSE
'Kathleen Harrop' [1919, Dickson, Northern Ireland], a sport from 'Zéphirine Drouhin', identical but for its softer, more pleasing colour.

OTHER RECOMMENDED ROSE
'Blairi No. 2' (Possibly *Rosa chinensis* x 'Tuscany') [1845, Blair, England] a medium-sized to tall climber, semi-double, large, pale pink, very fragrant flowers, a beautiful climber; and yes, there is a 'Blairi No. 1' but it isn't as good.

'Zéphirine Drouhin'

NOISETTES

On p.61, I described the origin in 1802 of 'Champneys' Pink Cluster' from a cross between *Rosa chinensis* and *Rosa moschata*. The man who discovered the cross in South Carolina was John Champneys and he gave the resultant plant to his friend Philippe Noisette. From its seedlings, Noisette selected a plant now known as 'Blush Noisette' and by crossing this in turn with other types of rose, he created the group that bears his name. They are all tall shrubs or climbers, with a delicacy of flower, a fine fragrance, a tendency to bloom rather later than most other old roses and a somewhat unfounded reputation for being tender.

'Madame Alfred Carrière'
(Unknown parentage) [1879, Schwartz, France]

❝ There really is no other large-flowered tall white climber to match this plant. It is extremely vigorous, flowers for a very long season, and has pretty well every other virtue that you could wish for apart possibly from its stems not being particularly pliable and, in consequence, sometimes tricky to train. It is ideally left to its own devices to grow up and over some large and unsightly object. ❞

FORM
Medium to tall climber.

FLOWERS
Double, large, loosely formed flower head, white with sometimes a slight touch of pink, moderately fragrant, repeat- to continuous-flowering.

HIPS
None.

SPECIAL FEATURES
The combination of vigour, flower colour and relative freedom from disease.

SHADE TOLERANCE
Moderate although prone to become twiggy.
WEATHER TOLERANCE
Moderate.
PRUNING – 1

OTHER RECOMMENDED ROSES

'Aimée Vibert' (syn. 'Bouquet de la Mariée', 'Nivea') (Possibly 'Champneys' Pink Cluster' x *Rosa sempervirens*) [1828, Vibert, France] a medium-sized climber, double, white, extremely fragrant flowers, almost thornless. Reliable, almost continuous-flowering after a late start but must be grown in a warm position.

'Céline Forestier' (Unknown parentage) [1842, Trouillard, France] a tall shrub or short climber, double, large pale yellow flowers with pink tinge, moderately fragrant, repeat-flowering, requires a sheltered spot to give of its best. In such a site the growth would be vigorous. Makes a good free-flowering climber.

'Desprez à fleurs jaune' ('Blush Noisette' x 'Parks' Yellow China') [1835, Desprez, France] a tall climber, double, small, yellow-apricot flowers, fairly fragrant, more or less continuous-flowering but always best in a warm spot.

'Madame Alfred Carrière'

TEA ROSES

Tea Roses today are best known as one parent of the Hybrid Teas but there are a few, all climbers, that I would never be without and include here. I don't, however, believe that any of the shrub varieties are indispensible other than for their historical interest. They first appeared in the 1830s as a result of crosses between, on the one hand, two of the old Chinese varieties of China Rose, 'Hume's Blush' and 'Parks' Yellow Tea Scented China' and, on the other, a range of Bourbons and Noisettes. And that name, 'Tea Rose'? It stems either from the fact that the first were brought to the West in the tea ships of the East India Company, or that their perfume has more than a hint of tea about it.

'Sombreuil' (Unknown parentage)
[1850, Robert, France]

" I searched long and hard for a white climbing rose of moderate vigour, a long flowering season and perfume. And I treasure the day when I found this variety, the answer to my prayer, for it has proved to have flowers of the most exquisite form, relative freedom from disease and complete hardiness. To the purist, it probably isn't truly a Tea Rose for one of its parents was probably a Hybrid Perpetual; but I care not, and in any event, if this perfume isn't tea rose perfume, I don't know what is. My mission is to spread this rose far and wide. "

FORM
Medium-sized climber.

'Sombreuil'

FLOWERS
Double, medium-sized, white, opening flat with the most superb, tightly crumpled centres, repeat-flowering.

HIPS
None.

SPECIAL FEATURES
A unique combination of qualities.

SHADE TOLERANCE Light or none.
WEATHER TOLERANCE Moderate to good.
PRUNING – 1

OTHER RECOMMENDED ROSES
'Niphetos' (Unknown parentage) [1889, Keynes, Williams & Co, England] a medium-sized climber, double, white, very fragrant flowers of charming form. Repeat-flowering but must have full sun and shelter as it is prone to damage by rain; ideally a rose for a large conservatory. 'Devoniensis' (syn. 'Magnolia Rose') (Unknown parentage) [1838, Foster, England] a medium-sized climber, very large, cream-white very fragrant flowers with a hint of pink, repeat-flowering, few thorns but must have full sun and ideally some shelter. The shrub from which this is a sport was the first Tea Rose to be raised in England.

TEA ROSES

'Gloire de Dijon' (syn. 'Old Glory') (Unknown Tea Rose x 'Souvenir de la Malmaison') [1853, Jacotot, France]

" *One of the half-dozen most beautiful roses in the world, eulogized in times past by the first president of the British National Rose Society, the Reverend Dean Hole, who called it 'the best climbing rose with which I am acquainted'. He went on to say, 'if ever, for some heinous crime, I were miserably sentenced, for the rest of my life, to possess but a single rose tree, I should desire to be supplied, on leaving the dock, with a strong plant of 'Gloire de Dijon'.' It has been eulogized more recently in the words of at least one popular song. It has that exquisite peachy colour that I love so much and yet it is a rose that can be rather tricky to grow to perfection as it is a poor performer in bad weather and can become twiggy if not carefully pruned. But all of the effort is always worthwhile.* "

FORM
Medium-sized to tall climber.

FLOWERS
Double, large to medium-sized, flat, wonderful peach-apricot coloured petals with subtle hints of pink, very fragrant, repeat-flowering.

HIPS
None.

SPECIAL FEATURES
Needs care and is prone to blackspot in some gardens (although not mine); it is suspected that the vigour of the stock varies from nursery to nursery.

'Climbing Lady Hillingdon'

SHADE TOLERANCE None.
WEATHER TOLERANCE
Poor.
PRUNING – I

OTHER RECOMMENDED ROSE
'Climbing Lady Hillingdon' ('Papa Gontier' x 'Madame Hoste') [1917, Hicks, England], another of the half-dozen finest roses. A medium-sized to tall climber, very long, pointed buds open to medium-sized, rather loose semi-double apricot flowers with very strong fragrance, repeat-flowering. Although always said to be slightly tender and sun-loving, mine thrives in a none-too-warm garden on a wall that does not receive sun throughout the day.

'Gloire de Dijon'

HYBRID PERPETUALS

These were the great shrub roses of Victorian gardens, hybrids as their name suggests and also with a long flowering season. But there is little other consistency among them save that one parent was very commonly a Bourbon. Unfortunately, because many were highly inbred, they lacked staying power and have disappeared. Many were also raised principally for their buds and flowers which were cut for show purposes, the form of the plant itself being rather neglected and, in consequence, they were often upright and of rather unappealing habit. Nonetheless, a few extremely attractive and worthy varieties remain.

'Frau Karl Druschki'

'Frau Karl Druschki' (syn. 'Snow Queen', 'Reine des Neiges', 'White American Beauty') ('Merveille de Lyon' x 'Madame Caroline Testout') [1901, Lambert, Germany]

" *This was the first white rose that I ever knew for it was my father's favourite and we grew it in my childhood garden; although in those days, it tended to be described as a Hybrid Tea (one of its parents, 'Madame Caroline Testout' is a Hybrid Tea). I've rediscovered its value in recent years although it isn't a good rose for wet summers and, sadly, lacks fragrance. But in flower form it takes some beating.* "

FORM
Tall, upright shrub (also climbing form).

FLOWERS
Double, medium-large, usually pure white, no fragrance, repeat-flowering.

HIPS
None.

SPECIAL FEATURES
Needs positioning with care because of its tall habit and will not be very exciting in wet summers.

SHADE TOLERANCE None to light.
WEATHER TOLERANCE Poor.
PRUNING – 1

POLYANTHAS

I think that the Polyanthas are among the unsung heroes of modern rose growing for their place in our gardens has largely been usurped by the smaller Floribundas that were derived from them, and more recently by the dreadfully named Patio Roses. Yet they have enormous historical interest as well as great charm. The Polyanthas (or as they are sometimes called, Dwarf Polyanthas) began in the second half of the nineteenth century with an accidental cross between a China Rose and *Rosa multiflora*, the parent of many Ramblers. The seedlings from this cross were very variable and only one produced seed. When this was sown in turn, its offspring were quite distinct: small continuous-flowering bushes with clusters of small flowers and from them were derived the Polyanthas that were so popular in the first half of the twentieth century. For convenience, I have included here also a few other beautiful small-flowered varieties that have many similarities to the Polyanthas but differ in such respects as their perfectly formed little flowers.

'White Pet' (syn. 'Little White Pet') (Sport from 'Félicité et Perpétue') [1879, Henderson, USA]

" Anyone wanting a dwarf white-flowered bush rose with at least some fragrance and a very long flowering season really need look no further. Fruitless hunting among the smaller Floribundas is quite unnecessary while 'White Pet' is available. I often wondered why it hadn't been used to intro-duce some of its characteristics into other varieties, but a leading rose breeder tells me that it obsti-nately fails to hybridize. "

FORM
Dwarf spreading bush.

FLOWERS
Double, small, flat white, large clusters, slight fragrance, continuous-flowering.

HIPS
None.

SPECIAL FEATURES
This rose really has few faults; it even has particularly lush green foliage to set off those perfect little flowers. In hot summers, its small, compact habit does, however, seem to encourage mildew.

SHADE TOLERANCE Light to moderate.
WEATHER TOLERANCE Moderate.
PRUNING – I

'Perle d'Or'

'Perle d'Or' (a Polyantha x 'Madame Falcot') [1883, Rambaud, France]

" This is one of the most admired roses in my garden for its exquisite little blooms, its peach-apricot colour and for its spirit, as it truly flowers its heart out all summer. It is, in all except colour, a carbon copy of that little button-hole rose, 'Cécile Brunner' and so similar are its flowers that I have never believed that they aren't, in reality, very closely related. "

FORM
Medium-sized, rather upright bush.

FLOWERS
Double, very small, of perfect 'Tea Rose' form, in large clusters, soft apricot-pink, slight fragrance, continuous-flowering.

SPECIAL FEATURES
The long, rather spidery flower stems are characteristic and shared, too, with 'Cécile Brunner'. Virtually dis-ease free in my experience.

HIPS
None.

SHADE TOLERANCE Light.
WEATHER TOLERANCE Moderate to good.
PRUNING – I

'Cécile Brunner' (syn. 'Madame Cécile Brunner', 'Sweetheart Rose', 'Maltese Rose', 'Mignon') (a Polyantha x 'Madame Tartas') [1881, Pernet-Ducher, France], identical in all respects to 'Perle d'Or' but with pale pink flowers. There is a very vigorous tall climbing form [1904, Hosp, USA] and also a white sport [1909, Fauque, France].
'Bloomfield Abundance' ('Sylvia x 'Dorothy Page-Roberts') [1920, Thomas, USA], very similar indeed to 'Cécile Brunner' but medium-sized to tall, the combination of size and the open, twiggy habit giving a very light and airy plant.

'Cécile Brunner'

'The Fairy' ('Paul Crampel' x 'Lady Gay') [1932, Bentall, England]

66 *If one rose sums up the virtues of the Polyanthas, then this must be it although, in truth, it does have an number of strange features. Its foliage is peculiar and it comes into flower later than virtually any other rose that I grow. But it has a reliability in almost all summers that is welcome, and it is certainly never short of flowers. It must, I suppose, be the most popular of all Polyanthas, although I wonder how many of those who grow it think it is simply an odd Floribunda.* 99

FORM
Dwarf to small spreading bush.

FLOWERS
Semi-double, small, loose, in large clusters, clear pink with gold anthers, slight fragrance, continous-flowering.

HIPS
None.

SPECIAL FEATURES
The late-flowering characteristic is a virtue rather than a drawback, for 'The Fairy' begins to bloom as many others are fading. It is also very weather resistant; an asset in damp summers. The leaves are extremely small and superficially not at all rose-like.

SHADE TOLERANCE
Moderate to almost deep.
WEATHER TOLERANCE
Good.
PRUNING – 1

'The Fairy'

'Paul Crampel' (Unknown parentage) [1930, Kersbergen, Holland], a dwarf to small rather upright bush; small, semi-double rich red-orange flowers in large clusters, little fragrance, repeat- or continuous-flowering; one of the first roses with this colour that is so popular today (although not with me).
'Gruss an Aachen' ('Frau Karl Druschki' x 'Franz Deegen') [1909, Geduldig, Germany], a dwarf to small, spreading bush, double, cream-white moderately fragrant flowers in small clusters; repeat- or continuous-flowering.
'Yesterday' (('Phyllis Bide' x 'Shepherd's Delight') x 'Ballerina') [1974, Harkness, England], a small, spreading bush, single or semi-double, purple-pink, moderately fragrant flowers in small clusters, few small roses have flowers of this form and colour, repeat- or continuous-flowering.
'Mevrouw Nathalie Nypels' (syn. 'Nathalie Nypels') ('Orleans Rose' x ('Comtesse du Cayla' x *Rosa foetida bicolor*)) [1919, Leenders, Holland], a dwarf to small, spreading bush, medium-sized salmon-pink flowers in large clusters, moderately fragrant, repeat- or continuous-flowering.

MODERN SHRUB ROSES

A Modern Shrub Rose is a flowering shrub, bred or discovered relatively recently (generally since 1945), that happens to be a rose. That's my definition and there is little more precision needed. The parentage of these roses varies widely, and includes Species, Hybrid Teas, Floribundas and sometimes older rose groups.

'Nevada' (Probably *Rosa moyesii* x 'La Giralda') [1927, Dot, Spain]

❝ One of the great Modern Shrub Roses, although in age only just 'modern' and surprisingly, from a country with little tradition of rose breeding. It has so much going for it: a fine shape, a strong constitution, few thorns and masses of flowers early in the season with good repeat-flowering. If you like the impact of huge numbers of simple flowers, and have the room, you will love this rose. ❞

FORM
Tall, upright to spreading shrub.

FLOWERS
Single or semi-double, cream-white with yellow stamens, appear in very large numbers, moderately fragrant, repeat-flowering.

HIPS
None.

SPECIAL FEATURES
This is a big plant and must be given room; may be prone to blackspot in wet seasons.

SHADE TOLERANCE None to light.
WEATHER TOLERANCE Moderate to good.
PRUNING – 1

RELATED ROSE
'Marguerite Hilling' [1959, Hilling, England] is a recent and very popular pink sport from 'Nevada' but otherwise similar in all respects.

'Frühlingsgold' ('Joanna Hill' x *Rosa pimpinellifolia*) [1937, Kordes, Germany]

❝ One of the earlier Modern Shrub Roses and probably the best and most popular of the 'Frühlings' series bred by Kordes. A well grown and mature plant of 'Frühlingsgold' is an imposing sight with its huge, thorny, arching stems. It makes a fine centre-piece to a large border, and mine is underplanted with the yellow poppy Meconopsis cambrica *which flowers at the same time, so complements it perfectly.* ❞

FORM
Tall, upright, arching shrub.

FLOWERS
Single to semi-double, large, in very large numbers, golden-yellow with yellow stamens, very fragrant, spring.

HIPS
None.

SPECIAL FEATURES
This is a very easy and carefree rose but a big one and also one with a short flowering season. It won't, therefore, earn its keep in a small garden.

SHADE TOLERANCE Light to moderate.
WEATHER TOLERANCE Moderate to good.
PRUNING – 1

'Nevada'

'Marguerite Hilling'

Of several others in this series with similar parentage, 'Frühlingsmorgen' (('E G Hill' x 'Kathrine Kordes') x *Rosa pimpinellifolia altaica*)) [1942, Kordes, Germany] is the best known although its rather sickly pink flowers with white and yellow centres and purple stamens aren't to everyone's taste.

'Frühlingsgold'

'Golden Chersonese'

'Golden Chersonese'
(*Rosa ecae* x 'Canary Bird') [1963, Allen, England]

❝ *This is an extremely beautiful rose that originated from a most interesting but rather obvious cross and I'm always surprised that it wasn't made sooner than the sixties. 'Canary Bird' is described on p.38 and the other parent,* Rosa ecae, *is another richly yellow-flowered although much smaller and very thorny shrub. Little wonder, therefore, that their offspring is a golden-flowered plant but it is one that has the great bonus of increased hardiness.* ❞

FORM
Medium-sized, upright, shrub.

FLOWERS
Single, small, in very large numbers, rich golden-yellow with gold stamens, strongly fragrant, spring.

HIPS
None.

SPECIAL FEATURES
The shoots are a fine rich brown colour and also very thorny; combined with the size of the rose, the fern-like, abundant foliage and a markedly upright habit, this makes for a very distinctive early season plant.

SHADE TOLERANCE Light to moderate.
WEATHER TOLERANCE Moderate to good.
PRUNING – 1

'Cantabrigiensis' (*Rosa hugonis* x *Rosa sericea*) [1931, Cambridge Botanic Garden, England], a medium-sized to tall arching shrub, with single, large yellow fragrant flowers in spring, brown thorny shoots and fern-like foliage. A lovely rose that, too, has affinities with 'Canary Bird' and could equally be placed on p.38.

'Chinatown' (syn. 'Ville de Chine') ('Columbine' x 'Clare Grammerstorf') [1963, Poulsen, Denmark], a medium-sized rather upright shrub, large double pale-yellow flowers with pink edging, very fragrant. Good weather resistance and a tough rose, repeat-flowering, sometimes classed as a Floribunda.

'Golden Wings' (('Soeur Thérèse' x *Rosa pimpinellifolia altaica*) x 'Ormiston Roy') [1956, Shepherd, USA], a medium-sized to tall, upright shrub, very large single yellow flowers with brown stamens and strong fragrance, unusual among single yellow shrub roses in its almost continuous-flowering. It is especially valuable on that count.

'Joseph's Coat' ('Buccaneer' x 'Circus') [1964, Armstrong & Swim, USA], a tall free-standing shrub or pillar rose, medium-sized, loose semi-double yellow and pink flowers with gold stamens and moderate fragrance, continuous-flowering. Thorny, upright plant with glossy foliage. If you like multi-coloured roses, you'll love it. If not, you won't.

MODERN SHRUB ROSES

'Jacqueline du Pré' ('Radox Bouquet' x 'Maigold') [1989, Harkness, England]

" *A rose named in memory of one of the finest musicians that England has ever produced must be a good one and this shrub lives up to that role. Having 'Maigold' in its parentage is a good start and although the only obvious inheritance from it is in the stamens, its good disease resistance came from there too. I have little hesitation in listing it among the best half dozen single flowered Modern Shrubs.* "

FORM
Medium-sized, spreading shrub.

FLOWERS
Single or almost semi-double, white, gold stamens, very fragrant, repeat-flowering.

HIPS
None.

SPECIAL FEATURES
Dark, lush foliage makes a fine foil for the flowers. Good disease resistance.

SHADE TOLERANCE None to light.
WEATHER TOLERANCE Good.
PRUNING – I

'Fred Loads' ('Dorothy Wheatcroft' x 'Orange Sensation') [1968, Holmes, England]

" *A rose for which I have a special affection as it is named after the late Fred Loads, one of my broadcasting predecessors. It has great vigour and large flowers. Strictly, I suppose it is a Floribunda, but it is a giant and more accurately classed as a shrub.* "

FORM
Tall, upright shrub.

FLOWERS
Single or semi-double, salmon-orange, yellow stamens in large clusters, barely fragrant, almost continuous-flowering.

HIPS
None.

SPECIAL FEATURES
A very strong-growing and disease-free plant; excellent for harsher gardens.

'Fred Loads'

SHADE TOLERANCE None to light.
WEATHER TOLERANCE Good.
PRUNING – I

'Bonica' (syn. 'Bonica '82') (Unknown parentage) [1982, Meilland, France]

" *I'm not quite sure why this rose has achieved such a large amount of fame, recognition and popularity as it does not seem appreciably different from a number of other roses either in its colour or habit. It's also Meilland's second stab at the same name, for he bred another rose called 'Bonica' some 30 years earlier. Nonetheless, with an Award of Merit from the Royal Horticultural Society, England, under its belt, it is clearly offering something worthy if slightly elusive.* "

FORM
Dwarf shrub.

FLOWERS
Semi-double, medium-sized soft pink with golden-yellow stamens and rather wavy petals, moderate fragrance and continuous-flowering.

HIPS
None.

SPECIAL FEATURES
I suppose the low-growing habit which makes this almost a Ground Cover rose is its really interesting feature, although the lush coppery-coloured foliage does set off the flowers.

SHADE TOLERANCE None to light.
WEATHER TOLERANCE Moderate.
PRUNING – I

'Fritz Nobis'
('Joanna Hill' x 'Magnifica')
[1940, Kordes, Germany]

❝ If only 'Fritz Nobis' had a longer flowering season, it would stand comparison with some of the finest roses. It does have many other attributes. Its petals have a delicacy that I find appealing and on looking closer you are rewarded with a hot, rich fragrance. ❞

FORM
Medium-sized to tall, upright shrub.

FLOWERS
Semi-double, medium, soft pink with yellow stamens, spicy fragrance, summer.

HIPS
Spherical, abundant, small, rich red.

SPECIAL FEATURES
The combination of characteristics is compelling, and not least the fine hips, relatively unusual in a Modern Shrub.

SHADE TOLERANCE Light to moderate.
WEATHER TOLERANCE Moderate.
PRUNING – 1

'Fritz Nobis'

'Nymphenburg' ('Sangerhausen' x 'Sunmist')
[1954, Kordes, Germany]

❝ The German rose breeder Wilhelm Kordes has many fine roses to his credit and although his fame in the area of Shrub Roses is centred on the 'Fruhlings-' series, there are some rose experts who consider this his greatest triumph. It is a big strong, healthy shrub yet with curiously delicate and charming flowers. I have seen it grown both as a free-standing Shrub and as a pillar rose and with the right companion plants, I think it is better with the support. ❞

FORM
Tall Shrub or Pillar Rose.

FLOWERS
Semi-double, medium-sized pink with hints of yellow, yellow stamens, moderate fragrance, continuous-flowering.

HIPS
After hot summers, top-shaped, red.

SPECIAL FEATURES
This is a very free-flowering plant and that, combined with the contrast between the strong bold foliage and the delicate blooms, is its real merit.

SHADE TOLERANCE None to light.
WEATHER TOLERANCE Moderate.
PRUNING – 1

'Cerise Bouquet'

'Nymphenburg'

OTHER RECOMMENDED ROSE
'Cerise Bouquet' (Rosa multi-bracteata x 'Crimson Glory') [1958, Kordes, Germany], a tall arching shrub or medium-sized Climber, double cerise-pink medium-sized very fragrant flowers, a very graceful habit on a big plant, summer.

ENGLISH ROSES

It is probably unique in the history of the garden rose that a new and distinctive group of varieties has arisen as a result of a deliberate and determined breeding programme. Yet such has been the origin of the so-called English Roses, thanks to the efforts of the English Rose breeder David Austin, who set himself the goal of combining the flower form and fragrance of some of the older shrub types with the repeat- or continuous-flowering characteristic so desirable in modern gardens. By crossing old with new varieties, he has succeeded to remarkable effect. The first rose of this type was probably the climbing 'Constance Spry' (1961), but the main launch came in 1969 since when almost 100 varieties have been released. I have selected those that are my own favourites and that, by and large, have proved the most popular. Most (including all those described here) are double flowered, none produces hips and none is significantly shade tolerant. They have moderate to good weather tolerance and should be pruned by Method 2.

'English Garden' (('Lilian Austin' x a seedling) x ('Iceberg' x 'Wife of Bath')) [1986, Austin, England]

" A truly exquisite rose, perhaps my favourite in the group for its wonderful flower colour and form. It is not so much the addition of the repeat-flowering feature that appeals to me; it is as if one of the old pink Shrub Roses with its crumpled petals had been dipped in paint of the loveliest golden-yellow. If you could have only one yellow Shrub Rose, this would not disappoint. I think it looks best when grown in a group of three or five surrounded with ground cover herbaceous plants. "

FORM
Dwarf to small, upright shrub.

FLOWERS
Double, very pale yellow with richer golden-yellow crumpled centres, moderately fragrant, continuous-flowering.

'English Garden'

'Graham Thomas' ('Charles Austin' x ('Iceberg' x a seedling)) [1983, Austin, England]

'Graham Thomas'

" Another fine yellow rose, taller than 'English Garden' but, for me, lacking its charm although it has been consistently popular since its introduction in the early eighties. The flowers are very different in form from those of the previous variety, having that characteristic cup-shape that has marked many good roses for centuries, but their fragrance is more modern and they lack that change in shade that I find so appealing.

Nonetheless, the strong rich green foliage displays good blackspot resistance, a blessing in any plant that produces yellow flowers, as they are particularly susceptible to disease. "

FORM
Small to medium-sized, upright shrub.

FLOWERS
Fully double, large, rich golden-yellow colour, cup-shaped, moderately fragrant, continuous-flowering.

'Abraham Darby'
('Yellow Cushion' x 'Aloha')
[1985, Austin, England]

❝ *Although the English Roses combine old and new virtues, this one manages it despite being the cross between two modern roses. The fact that one parent is 'Aloha', in many respects my perfect modern rose (p.117), is an excellent start although there is, at first sight, little of 'Aloha' to be seen for the flowers have an altogether older form although the coppery shades are familiar. It is a taller variety than many English Roses and I am told that it is rust-prone, although I have never seen it affected by this disease.* ❞

'Abraham Darby'

FORM
Medium-sized, upright shrub.
FLOWERS
Double, a beautiful apricot-flushed pink, medium-sized, more or less cup-shaped, very fragrant, repeat-flowering.

'Heritage' (a seedling x ('Iceberg' x 'Wife of Bath'))
[1984, Austin, England]

'Heritage'

❝ *Possibly the most popular of English Roses; the combination of flower form and colour, a more spreading habit and very few thorns gives it a special appeal. I have grown this rose for years and find it less weather-tolerant than some; there seems to be a slight weakness in the flower stalk when the blooms are full. But perhaps this is part of what is euphemistically called 'informality' these days.* ❞

FORM
Small, rather spreading shrub.
FLOWERS
Double, cup-shaped, soft pink, strongly fragrant, continuous-flowering.

'Country Living'
('Wife of Bath' x 'Graham Thomas')
[1991, Austin, England]

❝ *Like several of the later English Rose varieties, 'Country Living' is a cross between two earlier ones. It lacks fragrance but has charming, rosette-style flowers in a good old rose-pink, and is of a size that makes it suitable for many a modern garden. It is prone to shoot-death in colder gardens and shouldn't be planted in places exposed to cold winter winds.* ❞

FORM
Dwarf to small, upright shrub.
FLOWERS
Double, rose-pink with small, closed petals giving the form of a classic rosette, slight fragrance, continuous flowering.

OTHER RECOMMENDED ROSES
'Cottage Rose' ('Wife of Bath' x 'Mary Rose') [1991, Austin, England], a medium, upright shrub, double, pink, loose rosette flowers, slight fragrance, continuous-flowering. 'Mary Rose' ('Wife of Bath' x 'The Miller') [1983, Austin, England], a medium, spreading shrub, loosely double, pink flowers, fragrant, disease resistant, continuous-flowering; 'Winchester Cathedral' is white but similar in other respects. 'Gertrude Jekyll' ('Wife of Bath' x 'Comte de Chambord') [1986, Austin, England], a small to medium, upright shrub, large pink, fragrant flowers, continuous-flowering.

GROUND-COVER ROSES

The development of the ground cover plant has been one of the landmarks of gardening in recent years. The name is self-explanatory: they are low-growing, and so in a very literal sense, cover the ground with, at least in part, the objective of saving labour through suppressing weed growth. With the low-growing Ground Cover Roses, I'm not really sure how effective this is for they tend to be poor competitors and, since they are deciduous in most winters, they are at the mercy of weed growth in early spring. Their thorns also make them extremely unpleasant to work among if weed growth does become out of hand. Perhaps 'procumbent roses' or 'procumbent Shrub Roses' describes them better. Despite the problems, many of them are rather attractive plants. Few old roses fall into this category, and the majority are deliberately bred or selected recent varieties. Almost all attain about 60cm–1m (24in–3ft) in height and my designations of them as 'small', 'medium' or 'large' relate to their spread not, as in other sections, to their height. All should be pruned by Method 1.

'Ferdy'

'Nozomi'
('Fairy Princess' x 'Sweet Fairy') [1968, Onodera, Japan]

❝ I suppose this must be the most popular rose ever bred in Japan and it is certainly one of the most widely seen Ground-Cover Roses. In reality, it is a Miniature Climber although it is rarely grown in this way and its dense habit makes it more successful than many varieties at weed suppression. ❞

FORM
Medium-sized procumbent shrub.
FLOWERS
Small, single, silver-pink in large clusters, no fragrance, summer.
HIPS
None.
SPECIAL FEATURES
Desirable dense growth must be balanced against short flowering season.

SHADE TOLERANCE
Moderate.
WEATHER TOLERANCE
Good.

'Snow Carpet' ('New Penny' x 'Temple Bells') [1980, McGredy, New Zealand]

❝ This rose is unique, at least in my experience. I know of no other variety so small and neat with a creeping habit. It comes closest (in habit although not, of course, in origin), to being an Alpine rose and is, I think, the only rose that I would ever recommend for use in a rock garden. It is not useful ground cover in the conventional sense but is worthy of a place in any garden for its very special appeal. ❞

FORM
Tiny, creeping shrub, gradually forming a neat mound of growth.
FLOWERS
Very small, double, white, in large clusters, moderately fragrant (although you must be very close to the flower to detect it), repeat-flowering.
HIPS
None.

SPECIAL FEATURES
The size and habit are the appeal but against this must be set a tendency, as with other Miniature Roses (p.80), to shoot-death in winter.

SHADE TOLERANCE Light.
WEATHER TOLERANCE
Moderate to good.

'Snow Carpet'

OTHER RECOMMENDED ROSES

'Avon' ('Pink Drift' x a seedling) [1992, Poulsen, Denmark], a small procumbent shrub, small, very pale pink double flowers in large clusters, no fragrance, continuous-flowering.

'Paulii' (*Rosa arvensis* x *Rosa rugosa*) [1903, Paul, England], a large procumbent shrub, large single white flowers, yellow stamens, slight fragrance, mildew-prone, summer.

'Swany' (*Rosa sempervirens* x 'Mlle Marthe Carron') [1978, Meilland, France], a medium procumbent shrub, medium-sized double white flowers in large clusters, no fragrance, continuous-flowering.

'Norfolk' (Parentage not disclosed) [1991, Kordes, Germany], a small procumbent shrub, small, double yellow flowers, no fragrance, repeat-flowering.

'Sussex' (Parentage not disclosed) [1991, Poulsen, Denmark], a small procumbent shrub, small double apricot-pink flowers in large clusters, no fragrance, repeat-flowering.

'Rosy Cushion' ('Yesterday' x a seedling) [1979, Ilsink, Holland], a small, procumbent shrub, small semi-double, pink flowers in large clusters, slight fragrance, light shade tolerance.

'Ferdy' (a seedling climber x a 'Petite Folie' seedling) [1984, Suzuki, Japan], a small procumbent shrub, small, double salmon-pink flowers, no fragrance, continuous-flowering.

'Pink Bells' ('Mini-Poul' x 'Temple Bells') [1983, Poulsen, Denmark], a small procumbent shrub, small double vivid pink flowers in large clusters, slight fragrance, slight shade tolerance, summer.

'Macrantha Raubritter' ('Daisy Hill' x 'Solarium') [1967, Kordes, Germany], a medium procumbent shrub, semi-double, silver-pink flowers, quite fragrant, flowers in the summer; lovely but mildew-prone.

'Surrey' (Parentage not disclosed) [1987, Kordes, Germany], a medium-sized procumbent shrub, small, light pink double flowers in large clusters, no fragrance, some shade tolerance, repeat-flowering.

'Max Graf' (*Rosa rugosa* x *Rosa wichuraiana*) [1919, Bowditch, USA], a large procumbent shrub, single rich rose-pink flowers, moderately fragrant, summer; a lovely old variety.

'Red Blanket' ('Yesterday' x a seedling) [1979, Ilsink, Holland], a medium-sized procumbent shrub, semi-double, very deep pink flowers, slight fragrance, slight shade tolerance, may be prone to blackspot in some areas, continuous-flowering.

'Suffolk' (Parentage not disclosed) [1988, Kordes, Germany], a medium-sized procumbent shrub, single red flowers in small clusters, no fragrance, slight shade tolerance, repeat-flowering.

'Flower Carpet' ('Grouse' x 'Amanda') [1988, Noack, Germany], a medium-sized procumbent shrub, semi-double to double bright rose-pink flowers in large clusters, no fragrance, continuous-flowering.

'Nozomi'

MINIATURES AND PATIO ROSES

The development of Miniature varieties has arisen in many popular garden and indeed, house plants, a response presumably to the smaller size of most modern gardens (and modern windowsills). Roses are no exception although there have long been varieties with significantly small flowers and, in many respects, the whole process is a reversal of the long prevalent trend in gardening which has been to take small-flowered wild plants and selectively breed them for something larger.

The origin of the gene that confers dwarfness on most of the modern Miniature varieties isn't known for certain and there were several very small roses in the early nineteenth century that were grown largely as pot plants. It's thought, however, that a dwarf China Rose was the basis of the dwarfness although many of the early Miniature varieties that arose from it were lost. Then, in 1918, improbable as it sounds, an army medical officer called Dr Roulet discovered a plant in Switzerland that seemed to be a survivor. It was called *Rosa rouletii* and subsequently many rose breeders, most notably De Vink in Holland, Dot in Spain and more recently Moore in California, have used its progeny to produce a wide range of charming little plants of no more than 30 or 45cm (12 or 18in) in height and generally of fairly compact form, although sometimes rather taller and more leggy when in flower.

Miniature roses are generally slightly less hardy and weather tolerant than most normal-sized roses, they need little pruning apart from what I can best call tidying up (Method 4 p.24) but they may need more attention to pest and disease control. All are repeat- or more or less continuous- flowering and none has significant shade tolerance.

Patio Roses (how everyone seems to hate the term) are larger than Miniatures but smaller than Floribundas which they otherwise resemble. They have been developed largely by crossing the two groups and have become increasingly appreciated in recent years to the extent that four Patio Roses have received the British Rose Growers' Rose of the Year award. They are grown, pruned and otherwise treated in much the same manner as Floribundas (p.84) and like them, all are repeat- or continuous-flowering.

'Bright Smile'

'Easter Morning'
('Golden Glow' x 'Zee')
[1960, Moore, USA]

❝ *If there can be such a thing as a greatest Miniature, then this is it, Moore's finest little variety. Its combination of colour and the perfect form of its flowers add up to make it the Miniature that I'd grow if I could have no other.* ❞

FORM
Miniature bush, upright and compact, even in flower.

FLOWERS
Very small, fully double and of perfect Hybrid Tea form both in bud and when open, close to pure white.

'Easter Morning'

'Yellow Doll'
('Golden Glow' x 'Zee') [1962, Moore, USA]

❞ *This variety comes from the same cross as 'Easter Morning' and although it has good, well shaped flowers, they have nothing like the same quality. Its real merit is that it is the best yellow-flowered Miniature that I have grown, and although it is a fine plant, it must be said that the competition isn't particularly impressive. And sad to relate, it has inherited that familiar yellow China characteristic of susceptibility to blackspot.* ❞

'Yellow Doll'

FORM
Miniature, compact bush, remaining neat in flower.

FLOWERS
Small, double, neat but a little more open than those of 'Easter Morning', clear yellow, very slightly fragrant.

'Sweet Magic' (Parentage not disclosed)
[1987, Fryer, England]

❞ *The year 1987 was a good one for Fryers, the English rose breeders, for it yielded two Patio Roses that subsequently achieved the British Rose of the Year award. 'Sweet Magic' was the first, being granted the accolade in its first season, followed a year later by 'Sweet Dream'. The two are very different and this one has remained, I think, the more popular although it needs to be positioned with care. Once seen, the flowers are unlikely to be forgotten.* ❞

FORM
Patio, compact, low, rather spreading bush; its colour is really too assertive to use it as a dwarf hedge but it looks superb in containers positioned alongside a modern house.

'Sweet Magic'

FLOWERS
Medium, semi-double, in medium-sized clusters, golden-orange with an increasing hint of pink, moderately fragrant.

'Sweet Dream'
(Parentage not disclosed) [1987, Fryer, England]

❞ *My favourite peach-coloured Patio Rose and awarded the British Rose of the Year in 1988. Apart from the colour, it is the beautiful cup-shape of the flowers that catches the eye, together with fine lush green and largely disease-free foliage. I have grown this rose for several years and never yet seen mildew on my plants.* ❞

FORM
Patio, compact rather spreading bush, making it valuable as a dwarf hedge.

FLOWERS
Medium-sized, double, cup-shaped, peach-apricot, moderately fragrant.

OTHER RECOMMENDED ROSES
'Bright Smile' (Parentage not disclosed) [1980, Dickson, Northern Ireland], a Patio, compact, neat bush, medium-sized, semi-double or double, clear yellow flowers, slight fragrance, reasonable blackspot resistance for a yellow.
'Baby Masquerade' ('Tom Thumb' x 'Masquerade') [1956, Tantau, Germany], a Miniature, upright-bush, double flowers, changing from yellow to red as they open, slight fragrance.
'Cider Cup' (Parentage not disclosed) [1988, Dickson, Northern Ireland], a Miniature, rather spreading bush, small, double, neatly formed apricot flowers, no fragrance.

MINIATURES AND PATIO ROSES

'Darling Flame' (('Rimosa' x 'Rosina') x 'Zambra') [1971, Meilland, France]

❝ *This is a bit taller than most Miniatures and it also has flowers of unusually fine form for their colour. A friend who manages and owns a garden centre tells me that it has been in his top three best-selling Miniatures for many years, which proves, if nothing else, that a great many people like this colour a great deal more than I do.* ❞

FORM
Miniature, rather upright, relatively tall, taller still in flower.

FLOWERS
Small, semi-double to double, in large clusters, orange-red, slight fragrance.

'Darling flame'

'Top Marks' (Parentage not disclosed) [1991, Fryer, England]

❝ *British Rose of the Year in 1992, this is an outstanding little variety with a colour that is remarkably intense and durable with very little sign of fading. It is one of the best Patio Roses that I have grown for use in containers where it grows happily, showing no adverse reaction to the inevitable occasional drying out.* ❞

FORM
Patio, spreading but compact.

FLOWERS
Small, double, intense vermillion, not a great deal of fragrance.

'Dresden Doll' ('Fairy Moss' x a Moss Rose seedling) [1975, Moore, USA]

❝ *A remarkable variety, the first miniature Moss Rose (see p.46), but the fact that the cross is a difficult one to make explains why many others haven't followed. Even for a Miniature, it is very small; I will resist the temptation to say that its flowers are a bit out of proportion and add simply that it should be in every Miniature collection.* ❞

FORM
Miniature bush, neat, low-growing and compact.

FLOWERS
Small, semi-double to double, beautifully cup-shaped and fully mossed, soft pink, moderately fragrant.

'Dresden Doll'

'Gentle Touch' (a seedling x 'Memento') [1986, Dickson, Northern Ireland]

❝ *In 1986, this was the first Patio Rose to be named Rose of the Year. It is attractive, with very good colour, but Patio Roses were still relatively novel then and I'm not sure that it would win today. All the same, it is one of the Patio Roses that I see most often in gardens, rather than in catalogues.* ❞

FORM
Patio, low, rather spreading bush, a good container plant.

FLOWERS
Small, double, well formed in large clusters, clear pale pink, slight fragrance.

'Cricri' (('Alain' x 'Independence') x 'Perla de Alcanada') [1958, Meilland, France]

'Gentle Touch'

❝ *Relatively few Miniatures have come from the great French nursery of Meilland; this one has been with us for a very long time. But I have a confession about 'Cricri': I had a small bed of them in my garden for two or three years and then threw them out, although they were pounced on by a friend who transplanted them very effectively to his own garden and shows them with pride to all his visitors. I wasn't really sure about the colour and the flower stems had that rather leggy appearance that betrays their China ancestry.* ❞

'Angela Rippon' ('Rosy Jewel' x 'Zorina') [1978, de Ruiter, Holland]

❝ *In a world where rose varieties come and go with remarkable rapidity, and in a group with a flood of new names every year, it says much for this one that it has stayed the course and remained popular. I've grown it for many years and I have to say that I find it relatively unremarkable; trouble-free, certainly, but with a colour that is positive.* ❞

FORM
Miniature, medium-height, a slightly spreading bush, anaemic-looking foliage.

FLOWERS
Relatively large for a miniature, double, rich pink, slight fragrance.

'Angela Rippon'

FORM
Miniature, rather upright, medium-height, but much taller in flower.

FLOWERS
Small, double, in medium-sized, open clusters, an assertive coral-pink, little or no fragrance.

OTHER RECOMMENDED ROSES

'Pretty Polly' (Parentage not disclosed) [1989, Meilland, France], a Patio, spreading compact bush, small, double pale-pink flowers in large numbers, little fragrance.

'Queen Mother' (Parentage not disclosed) [1991, Kordes, Germany], a Patio, spreading bush, semi-double, clear pink flowers in medium-sized clusters, slight fragrance, notable for its good disease resistance.

'Tip Top' (a seedling x a seedling) [1963, Tantau, Germany], a Patio, low-growing, rather spreading bush, medium-sized, semi-double, rich, medium pink flowers in large clusters, little fragrance; everyone tells me that blackspot is a problem but I find it no worse than on many other Miniatures that I grow in my garden.

'Boys Brigade' (('Darling Flame' x 'Saint Alban') x ('Little Flirt' x 'Marlena')) [1983, Cocker, Scotland], a Patio, upright, compact bush, small, single, vivid red flowers with cream centres and brown stamens, lacking in fragrance. Rather distinctive and, in many ways, I find it preferable to some of the large-flowered Floribunda roses with their single red and white flowers.

FLORIBUNDAS (syn. Cluster-flowered Roses)

There can be no denying that, in the modern garden, the Floribunda reigns supreme. While I hope that there will be at least token representation of many other rose groups in everyone's collection, there is no other type of rose that offers so many flowers, for so many months, in so many different colours in return for relatively little care and attention and with relative simplicity of pruning. But of course, there are drawbacks. The flowers don't have either the perfection of form of the Hybrid Tea or the casual, timeless informality of the old roses. To be honest, most of them are a bit untidy. And while it is often asserted that 'modern roses have lost their perfume', this is a sweeping generalization and some Floribundas do indeed have a fine fragrance.

The Floribundas are simple in origin, most being the results of crosses between Hybrid Teas (p.94) and Polyanthas (p.70). Credit for their origin is due mostly to the Danish Poulsen nursery and the first crosses were made there before the First World War, but it was between the wars that the interest in them took off and by the middle of this century, they had become very important. The selection here is a personal one for the number of varieties now available is vast. But although there is variation within the group in many respects, there are three generalizations – all should be pruned by Method 2 (p.24), none produces hips worthy of the name and all are more or less continuous-flowering.

'Iceberg' (syn. 'Schneewittchen', 'Fée des Neiges') (Also a climbing form) ('Robin Hood' x 'Virgo') [1950, Kordes, Germany]

❝ The best white Floribunda ever raised and many rose growers would argue that it is the best of any colour. I remember that we grew its white Hybrid Tea parent, 'Virgo', in the garden when I was a child but when 'Iceberg' came onto the scene, at least half of the Virgos were tossed aside and replaced by this newer, finer specimen. Oddly enough, its virtues may come from the fact that it is an exception to the Floribunda rule for its other parent is a Hybrid Musk, one generation removed from a Polyantha. Probably the most reliable white rose of all time. ❞

FORM
Medium-sized, upright bush; taller than most Floribundas.
FLOWERS
Semi-double to double, white with brown stamens, moderately fragrant.
SPECIAL FEATURES
Best pruned lightly so it can be allowed to grow large enough to show off its shrub ancestry. Unfortunately, prone to mildew and blackspot.

SHADE TOLERANCE None to light.
WEATHER TOLERANCE Moderate to good.

'Allgold' (Also a climbing form) ('Goldilocks' x 'Ellinor Le Grice') [1956, Le Grice, England]

❝ Slightly older than many of Floribundas grown today, but still a beautiful rose and an important one that has been used extensively in breeding. It is the yellow Floribunda that I recommend above all others for its blackspot resistance and, although there may now be others as good, this remains an important virtue. ❞

FORM
Small, rather open spreading bush.
FLOWERS
Semi-double, clear buttercup-yellow of an outstanding clarity and durability, slight fragrance.
SPECIAL FEATURES
Lush foliage with high level of disease resistance.

SHADE TOLERANCE None to light.
WEATHER TOLERANCE Moderate to good.

'Iceberg'

'Amber Queen'
('Southampton' x 'Typhoon') [1984, Harkness, England]

" Two years after 'Mountbatten', the Harkness nursery had another British Rose of the Year triumph with 'Amber Queen', an outstanding rose for its colour. Despite the vigour of its parents, it is at the other extreme of size being a low-growing but neat plant. A classic rose if you like this shade. "

FORM
Small, compact bush.

FLOWERS
Double, amber-yellow, moderately to strongly fragrant.

SPECIAL FEATURES
Rich, lush foliage with reddish tints.

SHADE TOLERANCE None to light.
WEATHER TOLERANCE
Moderate to good.

'Mountbatten' ('Peer Gynt' x ('Anne Cocker' x 'Arthur Bell')) [1982, Harkness, England]

" To my mind, and to many other gardeners too, this has been the outstanding Floribunda of recent years in its combination of colour, fragrance and vigour. But make no mistake about the vigour; this is a massive rose, sometimes referred to as a yellow equivalent of 'The Queen Elizabeth' and almost a Shrub Rose in size. It isn't, therefore a plant for growing in a small garden, but it is a sine qua non for a big one. "

FORM
Medium-sized to tall, upright bush; taller than most Floribundas.

FLOWERS
Double, clear yellow, moderately to strongly fragrant.

SPECIAL FEATURES
Apart from the size, the high level of disease resistance is a real virtue. It is a plant that blends well with fresh green foliage shrubs and can be used for hedging.

SHADE TOLERANCE None to light.
WEATHER TOLERANCE
Moderate to good.

OTHER RECOMMENDED ROSES
'Margaret Merrill' (('Rudolph Timm' x 'Dedication') x 'Pascali') [1978, Harkness, England], a small to medium-sized bush, medium-sized double white flowers with a slight pink flush, borne in small clusters, exceptionally strong fragrance for a Floribunda, good disease resistance.

'Ards Beauty' (('Eurorose' x 'Whisky Mac') x 'Bright Smile') [1986, Dickson, Northern Ireland], a small, compact bush, large, very well formed double pale yellow coloured flowers, moderate fragrance, a fine, bushy rose with good disease resistance.

'Arthur Bell' ('Clare Grammerstorf' x 'Piccadilly') (Also a climbing form) [1965, McGredy, England], a small, rather upright bush, medium-sized semi-double rich, deep yellow flowers although fading rather depressingly, especially in rain or hot sun, moderate fragrance, good disease resistance.

'Champagne Cocktail' ('Old Master' x 'Southampton') [1985, Horner, England], a small, rather upright bush, medium-sized double yellow flowers with pink flecks, moderate fragrance.

'Amber Queen'

'Mountbatten'

FLORIBUNDAS (syn. Cluster-flowered Roses)

'Glenfiddich'

'Masquerade'
(Also a climbing form)
('Goldilocks' x 'Holiday')
[1949, Boerner, USA]

❝ Like the poor, 'Masquerade' will always be with us, although some people wish it wasn't. Many gardeners feel differently and adore it. To be truthful, in massed planting in parks, I can see that it has some virtue, but as a garden plant, only in other people's, please. ❞

FORM
Small, to medium-sized upright bush.
FLOWERS
Small, semi-double flowers in large clusters, at first yellow, then sickly pink, followed by red, all of the colours being present at the same time.
SPECIAL FEATURES
The colour is no longer unique as other varieties have joined it, but 'Masquerade' produces this mixture best; moderate disease resistance.

SHADE TOLERANCE
Moderate.
WEATHER TOLERANCE
Moderate.

'Glenfiddich' (a seedling x ('Sabine' x 'Circus')) [1976, Cocker, Scotland]

❝ One of the great Scottish roses and appropriately named. Its rich lush, whisky colour verges on the vulgar but just manages to avoid it. It is what I consider a very modern rose, a splendid subject for a modern house and garden. ❞

FORM
Small, upright bush.
FLOWERS
Medium-sized, fully double flowers of almost Hybrid Tea form, rich amber-orange, moderate fragrance.

SPECIAL FEATURES
Vigorous, very lush deep green foliage, and good disease resistance. I have, several times, seen this rose described as slightly tender which seems a very odd statement to make about a plant that has been bred in Aberdeen, a chilly, wind-swept city on the Scottish coast.

SHADE TOLERANCE None to light.
WEATHER TOLERANCE Moderate to good.

'Korresia' (syn. 'Fresia', 'Friesia', 'Sunsprite') ('Friedrich Worlein' x 'Spanish Sun') [1974, Kordes, Germany]

❝ There are many yellow Floribundas but 'Korresia' will always be among the top two or three and, yet again, it is an example of the outstanding achievements of Kordes. If I had one wish, it would be that it had that little extra richness that is present in the flowers of 'Allgold'; but on the other hand, it is better formed. ❞

FORM
Small, upright bush.
FLOWERS
Medium-sized, double flowers of almost Hybrid Tea form in small clusters, rich golden-yellow, moderate fragrance.
SPECIAL FEATURES
Strong and vigorous, good disease resistance.

'Korresia'

SHADE TOLERANCE Light.
WEATHER TOLERANCE Moderate to good.

'Harvest Fayre' (Parentage not disclosed) [1990, Dickson, Northern Ireland]

❝ British Rose of the Year in 1990 and of that strong shade of orange that the Scottish and Irish nurseries produce so well. It is a variety that first attracted my attention when I saw it in an inner-city planting scheme but with careful positioning, I have decided that it could be equally effective in small gardens if it was interplanted with something lush and green. ❞

FORM
Small to medium-sized slightly spreading bush.

FLOWERS
Medium-sized, semi-double or double rich orange-apricot flowers in large clusters, slight fragrance.

SPECIAL FEATURES
Apart from the vivid clarity of the colour, the rather late-flowering time is a merit as it continues fresh and clean well into the autumn.

SHADE TOLERANCE Light to moderate.
WEATHER TOLERANCE Moderate.

'Harvest Fayre'

'Southampton'
(syn. 'Susan Ann') (('Queen Elizabeth' x 'Allgold') x 'Yellow Cushion') [1972, Harkness, England]

❝ This variety crops up so frequently in the parentage of recent Floribundas that it must clearly have some special merits, as well as perhaps being somewhat promiscuous. I think, however, that the combination of size, colour and vigour that come from its own parentage is the real virtue, rather than any one character. ❞

FORM
Medium-sized, upright bush.

FLOWERS
Large, semi-double to double, in medium-sized clusters, peach-apricot with reddish flush, slight fragrance.

SPECIAL FEATURES
This is a big, vigorous and healthy looking plant that would perhaps benefit from a few more flowers; dark green foliage and good disease resistance.

'Southampton'

SHADE TOLERANCE
Moderate.
WEATHER TOLERANCE
Poor to moderate.

OTHER RECOMMENDED ROSES
'Anne Harkness' (('Bobby Dazzler' x ('Manx Queen' x 'Prima Ballerina') x ('Chanelle' x 'Piccadilly')) [1980, Harkness, England], a medium-sized, upright bush, almost a small shrub, semi-double to double apricot-yellow flowers, slight fragrance, fairly good disease and weather resistance. 'Golden Wedding' (Parentage not disclosed) [1990, Bear Creek, USA], a small to medium-sized bush, large, beautifully shaped double golden-yellow flowers, moderate fragrance, disease resistance; and what a way to guarantee sales with such a name. 'Tango' (seedling of 'Sexy Rexy') [1989, McGredy, New Zealand], a small, upright bush, semi-double, yellow and orange flowers in large clusters, slight fragrance; an interesting combination of flower form and colour.

FLORIBUNDAS (syn. Cluster-flowered Roses)

'Beautiful Britain' ('Red Planet' x 'Eurorose') [1983, Dickson, Northern Ireland]

" How curious that this Rose of the Year for 1983, so patriotically christened, should have as a parent the appallingly named 'Eurorose'. Perhaps it is poetic justice then that the parent never caught the public imagination in the way that this one has. To many gardeners, it will be just another more or less red Floribunda but I like it for its rather formal flowers and for that particular shade of red which adds interest. "

'Beautiful Britain'

FORM
Small, upright bush.

FLOWERS
Medium-sized, double flowers of almost Hybrid Tea form, rich orange-red, usually described as tomato red, slight fragrance.

SPECIAL FEATURES
Apart from the vibrancy of the colour of the flowers, which grows on you after some time, this variety has quite good disease resistance, although rather insipid-looking foliage.

SHADE TOLERANCE Light to Moderate.
WEATHER TOLERANCE Moderate to good.

'Melody Maker' (Parentage not disclosed) [1991, Dickson, Northern Ireland]

" Another Rose of the Year for Dicksons, this time in 1991 and once again, for a plant with those so-called Hybrid Tea-shaped blooms that have now become so important for the modern Floribunda. It's also another of those roses with a very modern colour, fine against a background of a modern brick house but not a rose for old stone-walled cottage gardens. "

'Melody Maker'

FORM
Small, rather spreading bush.

FLOWERS
Medium-sized, double flowers of Hybrid Tea form in large clusters, mid-vermilion red with some silvering within, slight fragrance.

SPECIAL FEATURES
A very good bedding rose that needs to be seen in a fairly massed planting; odd ones won't look right and the colour doesn't blend well with other varieties.

SHADE TOLERANCE Light to Moderate.
WEATHER TOLERANCE Moderate to good.

'Matangi' (a seedling x 'Picasso') [1974, McGredy, New Zealand]

❝ I must be honest and say that not many of the New Zealand McGredy roses appeal to me; I find them just too assertive and different from the older varieties from the Northern Ireland McGredy nursery. It's just as well for McGredys that I'm in the minority, for 'Matangi' was one of the most popular roses of the 1970s and has held its place since. ❞

FORM
Small, rather spreading bush.

FLOWERS
Medium, semi-double flowers of vivid red-orange with silver white in the centre and on the reverse, slight fragrance.

SPECIAL FEATURES
I find the problem with this type of rose is in knowing where to put it as no-one can pretend that it blends with much else. But it will turn heads.

'Matangi'

SHADE TOLERANCE Light to Moderate.
WEATHER TOLERANCE Moderate to good.

'The Queen Elizabeth' (syn. 'Queen Elizabeth', 'The Queen Elizabeth Rose') ('Charlotte Armstrong' x 'Floradora') (Also a climbing form) [1954, Lammerts, USA]

❝ This is one of the great Floribundas in a very real sense, for it is really shrub sized. I grow it at the back of a mixed border and prune it like a shrub; very little indeed. In consequence, it towers above most other things and, although it is scarcely beautiful when seen from the back, the finely shaped and coloured flowers sit superbly above the rather leggy stems and make a wonderful spectacle from the 'proper' side. It is interesting that what is usually thought to be a very English rose should have been bred in the USA. ❞

FORM
Medium-sized to tall, upright bush.

FLOWERS
Large, double, cup-shaped, fresh pink in medium-sized clusters, slight fragrance.

SPECIAL FEATURES
Apart from its size, which can work to its detriment, this is a remarkably adaptable rose, suited to almost all sites, including exposed ones; and it is highly disease resistant.

SHADE TOLERANCE
Moderate.
WEATHER TOLERANCE
Good.

'The Queen Elizabeth'

OTHER RECOMMENDED ROSES

'City of Belfast' ('Evelyn Fison' x ('Circus' x 'Korona')) [1968, McGredy, Northern Ireland], a small compact bush, medium-sized, very vivid orange-scarlet double flowers in large clusters, slight fragrance.

'English Miss' ('Dearest' x 'Sweet Repose') [1977, Cant, England], a small, compact bush, medium-sized, beautifully formed porcelain-pink flowers, slight fragrance; a neat Floribunda for cottage gardens.

'Many Happy Returns' ('Herbstfeur' x 'Pearl Drift') [1991, Harkness, England], a small spreading bush, pale rose-pink semi-double to double flowers, slight fragrance.

'Dame Wendy' ('English Miss' x 'Memento') [1990, Cant, England], a small, spreading bush, small, double rich pink flowers in large clusters, slight fragrance. A good modern rose for an old garden.

FLORIBUNDAS (syn. Cluster-flowered Roses)

'Elizabeth of Glamis'

'Elizabeth of Glamis'
(syn. 'Irish Beauty') ('Spartan' x 'Highlight') [1964, McGredy, Northern Ireland]

" This is a rose that tends now to be grown more for sentimental than horticultural reasons, as there are newer and better varieties of the same colour. Of the older Floribundas in my own garden, this is the one that probably requires most care and attention and I'm told that it isn't really a success in cold places; which is a pity as Glamis itself isn't exactly the warmest spot on earth. "

FORM
Small, upright bush.

FLOWERS
Medium-sized to large, double salmon-pink flowers in large clusters, with a moderate fragrance.

SPECIAL FEATURES
In my own garden at least, prone both to blackspot and mildew and in need of careful pruning as there is always a good deal of winter die-back.

SHADE TOLERANCE Light.
WEATHER TOLERANCE Poor.

'City of Leeds' ('Evelyn Fison' x ('Spartan' x 'Red Favourite')) [1966, McGredy, Northern Ireland]

" Rose catalogues describe this variety as 'reliable' which suggests that they can't think of much else to say about it. And to be truthful, nor can I, although it is popular with the rose-buying public. I grew it for a few years and it made a colourful enough display. "

FORM
Small, compact bush.

FLOWERS
Large, semi-double salmon-pink flowers, slight fragrance.

SPECIAL FEATURES
Reliable.

SHADE TOLERANCE Light to moderate.
WEATHER TOLERANCE Moderate to good.

'City of Leeds'

'Dearest'
(a seedling x 'Spartan') [1960, Dickson, Northern Ireland]

❝ *This is a lovely Floribunda with simple and, in some respects, rather old-style flowers. It has stayed the course because of this charm although I no longer grow it because, in my garden, it has become just too disease-prone. In warmer places, however, I would certainly still persevere.* ❞

FORM
Small, compact bush.

FLOWERS
Large, semi-double rose-pink, large clusters, moderate to strong fragrance.

SPECIAL FEATURES
The perfume is very good for a Floribunda but resistance to mildew and blackspot is less satisfactory.

SHADE TOLERANCE Light to moderate.
WEATHER TOLERANCE Poor.

'Dearest'

'Festival'
('Regensberg' x a seedling) [1994, Kordes, Germany]

❝ *A thoroughly modern Floribunda, British Rose of the Year in 1994, 'Festival' is vibrant, bicoloured and generally easy to grow. It surprises me that this rather crude rose comes from a nursery that has produced so many sophisticated classics in the past. It owes its colours to 'Regensberg' an extraordinarily vulgar bicoloured variety introduced by McGredy in New Zealand.* ❞

FORM
Dwarf to small, compact bush.

FLOWERS
Medium-sized, semi-double scarlet.

SPECIAL FEATURES
Good disease resistance and a great many flowers.

'Festival'

SHADE TOLERANCE
Moderate.
WEATHER TOLERANCE
Moderate to good.

OTHER RECOMMENDED ROSES

'Pink Parfait' ('First Love' x 'Pinocchio') [1960, Swim, USA], a small, upright bush; small, beautifully formed semi-double Hybrid Tea-style mid-pink flowers, large numbers of blooms in clusters of varying size; slight or no fragrance and good disease resistance.

'Anisley Dickson' (syn. 'Dicky', 'Munchen Kindl') ('Coventry Cathedral' x 'Memento') [1983, Dickson, Northern Ireland], a small, bush, large double, rich rose-pink flowers produced in large clusters, slight fragrance.

'Fragrant Delight' ('Chanelle' x 'Whisky Mac') [1978, Tysterman, England], a small, upright bush, large, semi-double pink-orange flowers in large clusters, strong fragrance; an extremely floriferous variety. Glossy reddish foliage.

'Piccolo' (Parentage not disclosed) [1983, Tantau, Germany], a small, upright bush, small, double red-orange flowers in large clusters, slight fragrance.

'Trumpeter' ('Satchmo' x a seedling) [1977, McGredy, New Zealand], a dwarf, spreading bush; double, vivid red-orange flowers produced in large clusters, slight fragrance, good disease resistance but does not stand up well to bad weather.

FLORIBUNDAS (syn. Cluster-flowered Roses)

'Evelyn Fison' (syn. 'Irish Wonder') ('Moulin Rouge' x 'Korona') [1962, McGredy, Northern Ireland]

❝ The early 1960s were good for the McGredy nursery, as they saw the introduction of both this rose and 'Elizabeth of Glamis' (p.90), two fine Floribundas that have held off the competition in the years since. I have a particular soft spot for 'Evelyn Fison' as there was a rather sad plant growing in the first garden that I ever owned and I nursed it through blackspot and back to health. By modern standards perhaps it is nothing spectacular but its colour is strong and fiery and doesn't fade. ❞

FORM
Small, upright bush.
FLOWERS
Medium-sized, double vivid red flowers in large clusters, slight fragrance.
SPECIAL FEATURES
The colour intensity is the outstanding feature of this rose and there is also moderate disease resistance.

SHADE TOLERANCE
Moderate.
WEATHER TOLERANCE
Moderate to good.

'Glad Tidings' (Parentage not disclosed) [1988, Tantau, Germany]

❝ British Rose of the Year in 1989, so this must be something special although I've never been quite sure why. It's a good enough variety with plenty of flowers and a strong colour and clearly people buy it in large numbers, but I just wonder how much of an improvement it is over the many other rich red Floribundas that have come and gone. ❞

FORM
Small, compact, upright bush.
FLOWERS
Medium-sized, semi-double rich crimson flowers that are produced in large clusters to make an abundant display, slight fragrance.

'Glad Tidings'

SPECIAL FEATURES
Flower quantity is perhaps the chief virtue of this rose together with slightly more perfume than you might expect from a red Floribunda.

SHADE TOLERANCE
Moderate.
WEATHER TOLERANCE
Moderate to good.

'The Times Rose' ('Tornado' x 'Redgold') [1984, Kordes, Germany]

❝ Yet another bright red, award-winning Floribunda but lower growing and neater than many, in my experience, with flowers of an unsophisticated but appealing rosette form. The best planting I've seen was in slightly mounded beds in front of a modern office block; the whole area seemed alive with colour. On a smaller scale, the effect could be created in front of a modern house. ❞

FORM
Small, rather spreading bush.
FLOWERS
Medium, semi-double scarlet flowers in large clusters, slight fragrance.
SPECIAL FEATURES
The habit is more spreading than that of its competitors but it is comparable in disease resistance and other respects.

SHADE TOLERANCE
Moderate.
WEATHER TOLERANCE
Moderate to good.

OTHER RECOMMENDED ROSE
'Lilli Marlene' (('Our Princess' x 'Rudolph Timm') x 'Ama') [1958, Kordes, Germany], a small, upright bush, medium-sized rich, velvety, deep red semi-double to double flowers in fairly large clusters, slight fragrance; a superbly coloured rose but flawed by susceptibility to disease.

CLIMBING FLORIBUNDAS

A number of bush Floribunda varieties have produced climbing sports over the years, but relatively few are as good either as their bush counterparts or as other climbing roses. There are, however, three notable exceptions in the climbing forms of 'Iceberg', 'Allgold' and 'Masquerade'. All should be pruned by Method 8 (p.25).

'Iceberg'

'Iceberg'
[1968, Cant, England]
(see p.84)

" All of the virtues and all of the mildew-prone vices of the bush form but with relatively few thorns on the climbing shoots and better shade tolerance. It is at best a short climber and for this reason makes an excellent pillar rose, quite superb when interplanted with a deep red-coloured clematis, such as 'Royal Velours'. "

'Allgold'
[1961, Gandy, England]
(see p.84)

" Of my three climbing Floribundas this is probably the least likely to stand the test of time, for there are now several other very good yellow climbing roses although the blackspot resistance of the bush form remains a valuable asset. It will become medium-sized to tall and is really a rose for a high wall or large tripod rather than a pillar. I no longer grow it for want of room but my recollection is that the perfume of the climber is better than that of the bush. "

'Allgold'

'Masquerade'
[1958, Gregory, England]
(see p.86)

" If, like me, you don't like the bush form of 'Masquerade', then the odds are that you won't like this tall, vigorous climbing version either. But apart from 'Handel' (p.114), there is probably no other climbing rose that produces quite so dramatic and colourful an impact. I know a fairly large country house with a sunny, sheltered wall covered from bottom to top with 'Masquerade' and there's no denying that passers-by stop and look. But it is a modern house and I'd hate to think anyone would do the same to old weathered stone. "

'Masquerade'

HYBRID TEAS (syn. Large-flowered Roses)

I can't deny that there is a snobbery attached to modern roses. Of the two great rose types of recent times, the Floribunda appeals more to what is euphemistically called the 'average' gardener who wants the maximum amount of colour and attractiveness in the garden in return for relatively little effort. By contrast, a gardener with the same criteria but who confesses to enjoying roses for their own sake will choose the Hybrid Teas, with their fewer although more perfectly formed flowers, generally stronger fragrance but, by and large, equal ease of cultivation. Personally, I've no time for horticultural snobbery and I grow what I believe to be the best roses of all types; the fact that generally I prefer the form of Hybrid Teas doesn't make them any better as plants or me any better as a gardener.

But what are the Hybrid Teas? Quite simply, they started out as hybrid roses of which one parent was a Tea Rose. The other parent, not immortalized in the group's name, was a Hybrid Perpetual and, like most hybrids, they combine the best attributes of each parent: at its simplest, the flower form and fragrance of the Tea Roses and the long flowering period of the Hybrid Perpetuals.

This is a personal selection from many hundreds. I have only included roses that I have grown or know, and while I must have overlooked many good varieties, selections from my list won't disappoint you. All should be pruned by Method 3 (p.24), none produces hips worthy of the name and all are more or less continuous-flowering.

'Pascali'
(Also a climbing form)
('The Queen Elizabeth' x 'White Butterfly') [1963, Lens, Belgium]

" I am among the many rose gardeners who consider 'Pascali' to be the best white Hybrid Tea that was ever raised, surpassing the strong claims of its recent rival 'Polar Star' (right). The vigour of 'The Queen Elizabeth' is evident, as is the superb flower shape that comes from having 'Madame Butterfly' in its ancestry too although, for the absolute purist, it must be said that the flowers, as with every other white Hybrid Tea, are seldom completely white, often possessing the merest hint of pink. "

FORM
Small, upright, somewhat lax bush in its growth habit.

FLOWERS
Medium-sized, double, with the unusual characteristic of being almost pure white, of very beautiful form with a slight fragrance.

SPECIAL FEATURES
The attractive flower form and colour will endear 'Pascali' to the rose buyer; the rather feeble fragrance, only moderate disease resistance and less than ideal bush form will just have to be tolerated for the sake of its assets.

SHADE TOLERANCE Light.
WEATHER TOLERANCE
Poor to moderate.

'Pascali'

'Polar Star' (syn. 'Polarstern') (Parentage not disclosed) [1982, Tantau, Germany]

❝ *This is really the rising star among white Hybrid Teas and was voted British Rose of the Year in 1985. But although the bushes are of better form than 'Pascali', I've watched it very closely through the past few summers, both wet and dry, and am not absolutely convinced that its flowers, although fuller, are of the same high quality. It is also, however, a vigorous plant, slightly taller than most Hybrid Teas although it cannot be determined from where in its parentage this vigour derives. Try it, but try 'Pascali' too.* ❞

FORM
Small, fairly compact, upright bush.

FLOWERS
Medium-sized, double, cream-white, no or slight fragrance.

SPECIAL FEATURES
The lack of fragrance is perhaps the final factor that prevents this variety toppling 'Pascali' from its perch but despite that, it is undoubtedly a very good, very neat garden rose.

SHADE TOLERANCE Light.
WEATHER TOLERANCE Poor to moderate.

'Polar Star'

OTHER RECOMMENDED ROSES
'Silver Wedding' (Parentage not disclosed) [1976, Gregory, England], a small, compact bush, slight to moderate fragrance, good disease resistance.
'Elina' ('Nana Mouskouri' x 'Lolita') [1985, Dickson, Northern Ireland], a small to medium-sized, compact bush, large double primrose-yellow flowers, slight fragrance; lovely but flowers rather sparse.
'The Lady' ('Pink Parfait' x 'Redgold') [1985, Fryer, England], a small, upright bush, large, double honey-yellow flowers with a pink flush, slight fragrance.
'King's Ransome' ('Golden Masterpiece' x 'Lydia') [1961, Morey, USA], a small, upright bush, medium-sized, double, deep golden-yellow flowers, slight fragrance, rather thorny and with a reputation for being fussy, but a lovely old variety with good blackspot resistance.

SHADE TOLERANCE Light.
WEATHER TOLERANCE Moderate.

'White Wings' ('Dainty Bess' x a seedling) [1947, Krebs, USA]

❝ *I have a very soft spot for single-flowered Hybrid Teas and have included several of them in the book. It's a great sadness to me that many gardeners don't even know of their existence. They became popular between the two world wars, although this one, one of the finest, is more recent.* ❞

FORM
Small to medium-sized, upright bush.

FLOWERS
Single, large, pure white with brown stamens, slight to moderate fragrance.

SPECIAL FEATURES
Simplicity, as with all singles, is the real merit. There aren't, in truth, very many flowers but each one is perfect.

'White Wings'

HYBRID TEAS (syn. Large-flowered Roses)

'Piccadilly'
('McGredy's Yellow' x 'Karl Herbst') [1960, McGredy, Northern Ireland]

'Piccadilly'

66 *The frequency with which 'Piccadilly' crops up as a parent of good modern varieties suggests that it has some special quality. It was one of the first two-coloured Hybrid Teas and its vivid tones still have tremendous appeal.* 99

FORM
Small, rather spreading bush.
FLOWERS
Medium-sized, double, vivid scarlet with yellow on reverse, slight fragrance.
SPECIAL FEATURES
Rich colours, a great many thorns and poor disease resistance.

SHADE TOLERANCE
Moderate.
WEATHER TOLERANCE
Poor to moderate.

'Grandpa Dickson' (syn. 'Irish Gold') (('Perfecta' x 'Governador Braga da Cruz') x 'Piccadilly') [1966, Dickson, Northern Ireland]

66 *To be fair, 'Grandpa Dickson' has certainly passed its peak in the popularity stakes and many other yellow roses, both Hybrid Tea and Floribunda, now out-sell it. But many gardeners, myself included, retain a very strong affection for it, not out of mere sentiment, but because of its very large, very well formed, graceful flowers, its reliability, and its impressive disease resistance, always a virtue in a yellow plant, as they are more susceptible to disease.* 99

FORM
Small, fairly upright bush.
FLOWERS
Large, double, pale lemon yellow with a slight fragrance.
SPECIAL FEATURES
Flower quality and disease resistance are excellent but the foliage is sparse.

SHADE TOLERANCE
Moderate.
WEATHER TOLERANCE
Moderate to good.

'Tequila Sunrise' ('Eurorose' x 'Typhoon') [1989, Dickson, Northern Ireland]

66 *I first saw this rose at the Chelsea Flower Show, London having been asked to introduce a television item while standing in front of it. It is one of the most striking of modern roses, but without the vulgarity that I associate with so many other bicoloured varieties.* 99

FORM
Small, upright bush.
FLOWERS
Medium, double, rich golden-yellow with scarlet edging, slight fragrance.
SPECIAL FEATURES
Unbelievably rich colours but the combination of gold and red doesn't have the same shattering impact as some of the modern orange varieties. Moderate disease resistance.

SHADE TOLERANCE
Moderate.
WEATHER TOLERANCE
Moderate to good.

'Tequila Sunrise'

'Peace'

'Freedom'

'Peace' (syn. 'Gloria Dei', 'Madame A Meilland', 'Gioia') (Also a climbing form) (('George Dickson' x 'Souvenir de Claudius Pernet') x ('Joanna Hill' x Charles P. Kilham') x 'Margaret McGredy') [1945, Meilland, France]

" *If not the greatest rose in the world, this is probably the greatest rose ever bred and certainly the most famous. It is undeniably a superb variety in its subtle colours, its fine flower form and its vigour. But it is also endearing in its unpredictability, for it varies greatly in performance and effect from garden to garden, and it has drawbacks, most notably a feeble perfume. It's impossible now to ponder how much of its reputation is based on its inherent qualities and how much on its being in the right place at the right time. It was bred by Meilland in the 1930s and although the Second World War put a stop to commercial development, three batches of cuttings were slipped out of France in 1942. The name 'Peace' was conferred at the Convention of the Pacific Rose Society in California on the day in 1945 that Berlin fell to the Allies.* "

FORM
Medium-sized upright bush or medium-sized shrub if only lightly pruned.

FLOWERS
Large, double, pale yellow with pink flush, cup-shaped when open gradually fading but variable in their intensity, slight fragrance.

SPECIAL FEATURES
Stature, in every sense of the word and, I think, best grown as a semi-shrub. Vigorous with good disease resistance.

SHADE TOLERANCE Poor to moderate.
WEATHER TOLERANCE Moderate to good.

RELATED ROSE
'Chicago Peace' [1962, Johnston, USA] is a lovely and interesting sport, which is virtually identical in appearance to its famous parent but with much more warm pink and coppery tones to dominate the yellow effectively. There is also a rose called 'Pink Peace', not to be confused with it, which simply has 'Peace' in its parentage.

OTHER RECOMMENDED ROSES
'McGredy's Yellow' (Also a climbing form) (('Mrs Charles Lamplough' x ('The Queen Alexandra Rose' x J B Clark')) [1934, McGredy, Northern Ireland], a small, compact bush, medium-sized, double primrose-yellow flowers, slight fragrance, good disease resistance.
'Freedom' (Parentage not disclosed) [1984, Dickson, Northern Ireland], a small compact bush, medium-sized, double rich yellow flowers, moderate fragrance; good disease and weather tolerance and one of the tougher, yellow Hybrid Teas that is available.
'Spek's Yellow' (Also a climbing form) (syn. 'Golden Sceptre') ('Golden Rapture' x a seedling) [1950, Spek, Holland], a small, upright bush, medium-sized, double though rather loose, rich golden-yellow flowers, moderate fragrance, a lovely colour but best given a little shelter.

HYBRID TEAS (syn. Large-flowered Roses)

'Mrs Oakley Fisher'
(Unknown parentage) [1921, Cant, England]

❝ Possibly my favourite among a favourite group of single Hybrid Teas, this is a rose of surpassing beauty, but it needs careful positioning for it will be lost among others in a large bed. A group of three is ideal placed together, in a prominent place with a lush green background and perhaps surrounded by amber-coloured gravel. Once seen, grown as it should be, this rose will never be forgotten. ❞

FORM

Small, spreading, open bush.

FLOWERS

Large, single, apricot-yellow with red-brown centre and amber stamens, moderate fragrance.

SPECIAL FEATURES

No other single-flowered rose that I can think of has flowers of quite this colour and beauty. Disease resistance is good too.

SHADE TOLERANCE Light to moderate.
WEATHER TOLERANCE Moderate.

'Mrs Oakley Fisher'

'Just Joey' ('Fragrant Cloud' x 'Dr A J Verhage') [1972, Cant, England]

❝ I adore this rose which has an appealing simplicity almost on a par with the single-flowered varieties of which I'm so fond. It can't be coincidence that it is from the same nursery that produced 'Mrs Oakley Fisher' (above) 50 years earlier. Like the singles, it isn't a typical Hybrid Tea with its loose flowers and their ragged petals, but the combination of this lightness of appearance with a charming colour means that it has endured and will continue to do so. ❞

SHADE TOLERANCE
Moderate.
WEATHER TOLERANCE
Moderate to good.

FORM
Small, upright compact bush.
FLOWERS
Medium, double, pale copper-orange with paler edges, moderate fragrance.
SPECIAL FEATURES
The flowers are unique and disease resistance is good.

'Just Joey'

'Rosemary Harkness'

'Whisky Mac'
(Parentage not disclosed)
[1967, Tantau, Germany]

'Whisky Mac'

❝ *The first time I saw 'Whisky Mac', I felt it was a potential champion. Indeed, it has proved a popular seller and I see it in many gardens. What will prevent it being a world beater, is that it is simply not strong-growing or tough enough. But its colour and perfume will always draw admirers.* ❞

FORM
Small, upright and rather open bush.

FLOWERS
Medium-sized, double, amber-gold, strong fragrance.

SPECIAL FEATURES
Disease resistance is poor and growth can be weak, especially in less than perfect growing conditions. A rose for good, warm soils.

SHADE TOLERANCE
Moderate.
WEATHER TOLERANCE Poor.

'Sutter's Gold' (Also a climbing form)
('Charlotte Armstrong' x 'Signora') [1950, Swim, USA]

❝ *Another elderly Hybrid Tea and another yellow that I have long recommended as blackspot resistant. I haven't grown it for several years so don't know if the resistance is still as good. It's a rose that I used to see a great deal of at the village flower show when I was a boy and I seem to recall that the very beautiful elongated flowers and reddish markings regularly took the judges' eyes.* ❞

'Sutter's Gold'

FORM
Small, upright but rather open bush in its growth habit.

FLOWERS
Large, double, deep yellow with hints of pink and reddish veins, moderate to strong fragrance.

SPECIAL FEATURES
The veining on the flowers is fairly unusual in rose cultivars developed today although it was a feature of a number of the Hybrid Teas of the immediate post-war period. I find it an attractive feature although there's no denying that if it is clear, unadulterated yellow that you want, this isn't for you.

SHADE TOLERANCE
Moderate.
WEATHER TOLERANCE
Moderate to good.

OTHER RECOMMENDED ROSES

'Rosemary Harkness' (Parentage not disclosed) [1985, Harkness, England], a small, spreading bush, medium-sized, double orange-yellow flowers with pink flush, quite fragrant, good disease resistance. 'Apricot Silk' ('Souvenir de Jacques Verschuren' x unknown variety) [1965, Gregory, England], a small, spreading bush, large, double apricot flowers with silky texture, slight fragrance, disease prone but unique colour and appearance. 'Bettina' (Also a climbing form) (('Peace' x ('Madame Joseph Perraud' x 'Demain')) [1953, Meilland, France], a small, compact bush, medium-sized, double orange flowers with the darker veining that was popular at the time, slight fragrance, a lovely rose but blackspot-prone and in need of weather protection. 'Troika' (syn. 'Royal Dane') (Parentage not disclosed) [1971, Poulsen, Denmark], a small, spreading, compact bush, large, double, rich orange flowers with hints of red, slight fragrance, a very strong-growing and disease resistant rose.

HYBRID TEAS (syn. Large-flowered Roses)

'Dawn Chorus'
(Parentage not disclosed) [1993, Dickson, Northern Ireland]

It's relatively infrequent these days for a Hybrid Tea to beat off the challenges of Floribundas and Patio Roses to take the British Rose of the Year award, but 'Dawn Chorus' did just that in 1993 so it must provide something special. I suppose it does, although it joins a large group of orange modern varieties without having anything extraordinary to offer, although the flowers do have a fine form.

FORM
Small, spreading but compact bush.

FLOWERS
Medium-sized, double, orange flowers, with a hint of yellow, slight fragrance.

SPECIAL FEATURES
Good disease resistance and a neat, compact habit.

SHADE TOLERANCE
Moderate.

WEATHER TOLERANCE
Moderate to good.

'Dawn Chorus'

'Remember Me'
('Alexander' x 'Silver Jubilee') [1984, Cocker, Scotland]

This variety caused quite a stir when it was first introduced in the eighties, partly because of its colour but mainly because of the fact, stressed by its raiser, that it could be classed either as a Floribunda or a Hybrid Tea, having flowers of fine form but borne in large clusters. It does, however, have good solid Hybrid Tea parentage on both sides.

FORM
Small, upright bush.

FLOWERS
Medium-sized, double, rich copper-orange flowers with a flush of yellow, of fine form and borne in small clusters, moderate fragrance.

SPECIAL FEATURES
Unique habit, very unusual colour, good disease resistance; certain to endure.

SHADE TOLERANCE
Moderate.

WEATHER TOLERANCE
Good.

'Remember Me'

'Dainty Bess'
('Ophelia' x 'K of K') [1925, Archer, England]

Another gem among the singles, one of the rather large group that was raised between the wars and one of few to have survived. It is the parent of other fine varieties but, as with most of them, it must be given a place of its own if it is to succeed as it should. Apart from its beautiful colour, the petals are most endearingly fringed.

FORM
Small, upright bush.

FLOWERS
Large, single, rose-pink with fringed edges, moderate fragrance.

SPECIAL FEATURES
Apart from the appeal of the single flowers, this has the best fragrance of any single Hybrid Tea that I have grown.

SHADE TOLERANCE
Moderate.

WEATHER TOLERANCE
Poor to moderate.

'Dainty Bess'

'Super Star' (syn. 'Tropicana') (Also a climbing form) ((a seedling x 'Peace') x (a seedling x 'Alpine Glow')) [1960, Tantau, Germany]

" This really was the bright star of its time, the first Hybrid Tea with this colour and, in consequence, it appeared in everyone's gardens and picked up every award going; including high recommendation for disease resistance. How things change, however, and I always cite the story of 'Super Star' as an example of the way that resistance to disease may not last. It altered badly for 'Super Star' and you will be lucky now to find a plant free from mildew; but it does still have many fans; presumably ones with long memories. "

FORM
Small, upright bush.

FLOWERS
Medium-sized heads, double, orange-vermillion, slight fragrance.

SPECIAL FEATURES
The colour is still striking, if no longer unique but disease is likely to be many gardeners' most striking impression of it today.

SHADE TOLERANCE
Moderate.

WEATHER TOLERANCE
Moderate to good.

OTHER RECOMMENDED ROSES

'Alexander' (syn. 'Alexandra') ('Super Star' x ('Anne Elizabeth' x 'Allgold')) [1972, Harkness, England], a medium-sized bush or shrub, medium-sized double, intensely vermillion flowers, slight fragrance, good disease and weather resistance; a rose that has taken much of the glory from its parent 'Super Star'.

'Cheshire Life' ('Prima Ballerina' x 'Princess Michiko') [1972, Fryer, England], a small, upright bush, large double, vermillion-orange flowers of very fine form, little fragrance, very good disease resistance and weather tolerance.

'Doris Tysterman' ('Peer Gynt' x a seedling) [1975, Wisbech Plant Co, England], a small, upright bush, medium-sized, double, copper-orange flowers, slight fragrance, poor disease resistance but a good colour.

'Lover's Meeting' (a seedling x 'Egyptian Treasure') [1980, Gandy, England], a small, upright bush, medium-sized, double, vermillion-orange flowers, slight fragrance and good disease resistance.

'Super Star'

HYBRID TEAS (syn. Large-flowered Roses)

'Ophelia' (Also a climbing form) (Probably a seedling of 'Antoine Rivoire') [1912, Paul, England]

❝ I suppose it's inevitable that plants one knew as a child create the most abiding impression; and so it is with 'Ophelia' and its sport 'Madame Butterfly', which were favourites in our garden. They are among the earliest of the 'modern' Hybrid Teas to have survived and are varieties that are said to have lost something of their former vigour although, unless my memory is playing me false, mine today are as good as those that I remember. But it will pay to see the plants growing before you place your order as different nurseries may well have stock of different vigour. ❞

FORM
Small, upright bush.

FLOWERS
Medium-sized, double, soft pink with slight yellowing at the base of the petals, very fragrant.

SPECIAL FEATURES
The combination of flower colour and perfume are endearing, although the disease resistance is no more than you would expect of an old variety.

SHADE TOLERANCE
Moderate.

WEATHER TOLERANCE
Poor to moderate.

'Ophelia'

RELATED ROSES
'Madame Butterfly' [1918, Hill, USA], 'Lady Sylvia' [1926, Stevens, England] and 'Westfield Star' [1922, Morse, England] are all sports from 'Ophelia', and are, respectively, slightly deeper pink, pinkish-peach and cream-white. I still think 'Madame Butterfly' the loveliest of a lovely group but in all other respects, they are identical.

'Picture' (Also a climbing form) (Unknown parentage) [1932, McGredy, Northern Ireland]

❝ Another beautiful Hybrid Tea from the past; you can see it just gazing at you from the pages of pre-war rose catalogues and it seems in a different world to some of the modern varieties that have usurped its popularity. It's a rose that I like to think a traditional old-fashioned lover of roses would never be without; although I do think that a little more fragrance would be welcome. ❞

SHADE TOLERANCE
Moderate.

WEATHER TOLERANCE
Moderate.

FORM
Small, upright and rather open bush.

FLOWERS
Small, double, rose-pink, slight fragrance.

SPECIAL FEATURES
A simple timelessness best describes the feel of this rose, although its disease resistance isn't particularly good.

'Picture'

'Betty Uprichard' (Unknown parentage) [1922, Dickson, Northern Ireland]

❝ *A variety that comes from a time when fragrance was expected, if not taken for granted, colours were soft and diseases were just one of those things that rose gardeners had to put up with. And it comes too from a time when, according to many rose experts, the old established Dickson nursery was at the height of its powers, when many of their roses, this one included, picked up National Rose Society awards on their way to fame and popularity.* ❞

FORM
Small, upright bush.

FLOWERS
Medium-sized, semi-double, salmon-pink with darker, rose-pink reverses to the petals, strong fragrance.

SPECIAL FEATURES
Very fragrant; mildew-prone.

SHADE TOLERANCE
Moderate.

WEATHER TOLERANCE
Moderate.

'Home Sweet Home'

'Prima Ballerina' (syn. 'Premiere Ballerine') (a seedling x 'Peace') [1958, Tantau, Germany]

❝ *How hard 'Peace' has worked as a parent for other varieties; and although not all have lived up to the expectations that such a pedigree might raise, this one certainly has and there are still many rose growers who would argue its case as among the best of all pink Hybrid Teas. For me, it would need bigger and better formed flowers to receive that accolade but it remains a first class rose.* ❞

FORM
Small, upright bush.

FLOWERS
Medium-sized, double, becoming rather loose, rich rose-pink, strong fragrance.

SPECIAL FEATURES
Very fragrant; mildew-prone.

'Prima Ballerina'

SHADE TOLERANCE
Moderate.

WEATHER TOLERANCE
Moderate.

OTHER RECOMMENDED ROSES
'Home Sweet Home' (Unknown parentage) [1941, Wood & Ingram, England], a small, upright bush, large, almost spherical, rich rose-pink flowers, strong fragrance, good disease resistance; also has a very good climbing form that I know better. It is a medium-sized climber and has large, double, markedly spherical flowers of a rich rose-pink with a strong fragrance. Good disease resistance.
'Savoy Hotel' ('Silver Jubilee' x 'Amber Queen') [1989, Harkness, England], a small, upright bush, medium-sized double, clear, pale pink flowers, slight fragrance; rather good, dark foliage that contrasts well with the flowers.
'Congratulations' (syn. 'Sylvia') ('Carina' x a seedling) [1978, Kordes, Germany], a small, upright bush, medium-sized, double, soft rose-pink flowers, slight fragrance, good disease resistance and weather tolerance.

HYBRID TEAS (syn. Large-flowered Roses)

'Fragrant Cloud' (syn. 'Duftwolke', 'Nuage Parfumé') (a seedling x 'Prima Ballerina') [1964, Tantau, Germany]

'Fragrant Cloud'

Given a rose with a name like 'Fragrant Cloud', everyone will know something of its virtues. The rest is, at best, a surprise and, at worst, a let down because you just don't expect roses with colour of this intensity to be fragrant. I am the first to admit that I like perfumed roses, but personally I'm not prepared to suffer the very lurid red of this rose in order to have them.

FORM
Small, upright bush.

FLOWERS
Large, double, tomato-red, very fragrant.

SPECIAL FEATURES
The colour and the perfume say all there is to say about this rose.

SHADE TOLERANCE
Moderate.

WEATHER TOLERANCE
Moderate to good.

'Silver Jubilee' ((a seedling x 'Parkdirektor Riggers' x 'Piccadilly') x 'Mischief') [1978, Cocker, Scotland]

Once in a while a rose comes along that everyone recognizes as a triumph and, whatever else the Cocker nursery produces, this variety alone will ensure their fame. It has collected numerous awards and, in a relatively short time, has won admirers among gardeners and rose breeders. Of course, it also came at an opportune moment to be named in honour of Queen Elizabeth II's Silver Jubilee. Its parentage is most interesting, including a most improbable progenitor in the semi-double and bold-red climber 'Parkdirektor Riggers'. From somewhere have come flowers of the most divine form.

FORM
Small, rather spreading but also compact bush.

FLOWERS
Large, double, of perfect form, silver-pink and apricot with darker reverses to the petals, very fragrant.

SPECIAL FEATURES
Flowers of the most splendid form, unfading colours, very good rich, glossy foliage and an extremely high level of disease resistance.

SHADE TOLERANCE
Moderate.

WEATHER TOLERANCE
Moderate to good.

'Silver Jubilee'

'Double Delight'
('Granada' x 'Garden Party') [1977, Swim & Ellis, USA]

Even in a world where bicoloured and painted roses have become more or less universally accepted, if not desired, this one takes some beating. I can't pretend that I like it but I recommend it as one of the best of its kind for those who do. I have something of an aversion to picotee flowers of what ever kind but at least, if you close your eyes, this one does offer a pleasant nasal experience.

SHADE TOLERANCE
Moderate.
WEATHER TOLERANCE
Moderate to good.

FORM
Small, upright bush.
FLOWERS
Large, double, white with cream centre and pinkish-red edges; very fragrant.
SPECIAL FEATURES
My comments about 'Fragrant Cloud' apply here too; only even more so.

'Double Delight'

'Alec's Red' ('Fragrant Cloud' x 'Dame de Couer') [1970, Cocker, Scotland]

'Alec's Red'

Alec Cocker was an outstanding rose breeder and if 'Silver Jubilee' was his greatest triumph, it's appropriate that this variety, arguably the finest red rose ever raised, should bear his name. Put beside 'Fragrant Cloud', its superiority is evident. Yes, red roses can and should be fragrant; but whether they appeal to me hinges on the quality of the red.

FORM
Small, upright bush.
FLOWERS
Very large, double, rather spherical in form, rich cherry-red, very fragrant.

OTHER RECOMMENDED ROSES
'Paul Shirville' (syn. 'Heart Throb') ('Compassion' x 'Mischief') [1983, Harkness, England], a small, upright bush, large, double fresh pink flowers with peach colour at base of petals, very fragrant.
'Blessings' ('The Queen Elizabeth' x a seedling) [1967, Gregory, England], a small, upright bush, medium-sized, double coral pink flowers, slight fragrance, good disease resistance.
'Wendy Cussons' ('Independence' x 'Eden Rose') [1963, Gregory, England], a small, spreading bush, large double, deep rose-pink flowers, very fragrant, a very good rose with excellent weather tolerance – but unfortunately spoiled by poor disease resistance.
'Rose Gaujard' ('Peace' x a seedling of 'Opera') [1957, Gaujard, France], a small, spreading bush, large, double, rich rose-red petals with silver-white on the reverse side, slight fragrance, good disease resistance and weather tolerance, but just not to my taste although many gardeners love it, so I have included it for their sake.

SPECIAL FEATURES
Yes, probably the best red rose ever bred; certainly the best red Hybrid Tea that is available, and with good disease resistance too.

SHADE TOLERANCE
Moderate.
WEATHER TOLERANCE
Moderate to good.

HYBRID TEAS (syn. Large-flowered Roses)

'Ena Harkness' (Also a climbing form) ('Crimson Glory' x 'Southport') [1946, Norman, England]

❝ Albert Norman was one of the great amateur rose breeders, and visitors to my garden are always grateful to him, for one of the first plants that they see on their arrival is 'Ena Harkness' on the front wall of my house. This is the climbing form (see p.113) and it is probably slightly better grown in this way than as a bush. But those rich dark flowers were one of the glories of the rose garden scene in the immediate post-war years; and I'm delighted that in some gardens at least, they have remained so. ❞

FORM

Small, rather spreading bush.

FLOWERS

Large, double, of beautiful and classic form, velvety crimson, very fragrant.

SPECIAL FEATURES

The rich colour and texture of the flowers; a tendency for the flowers to hang their heads is often referred to as a drawback but it isn't a serious one. Good disease resistance.

SHADE TOLERANCE Good.
WEATHER TOLERANCE
Moderate to good.

'Ena Harkness'

'Ernest H. Morse' (also a climbing form) (Unknown parentage) [1964, Kordes, Germany]

❝ I have a suspicion that this good old rose may at last be on the decline, for I see it in fewer and fewer catalogues, presumably because it is becoming increasingly prone to mildew. This is a shame for it has many virtues, partly in its good colour but also in its strong upright growth. If you are prepared to take a little extra care with it, it is worth the effort. ❞

'Ernest H. Morse'

FORM

Small, upright, compact bush.

FLOWERS

Large, double, bright crimson coloured and very fragrant.

SPECIAL FEATURES

The combination of strong unfading colour with strong growth is not a common feature among red-flowered bush roses.

SHADE TOLERANCE
Moderate to good.
WEATHER TOLERANCE
Moderate to good.

'Harry Wheatcroft' (Sport from 'Piccadilly')
[1972, Wheatcroft, England]

" It's always been a mystery to me why that great rosarian, the late Harry Wheatcroft should have chosen this, of all varieties to carry his name into perpetuity. I can only assume that he must have liked it. I don't, but then I know that I am in the minority. There's certainly nothing else remotely similar and I suppose that, on those grounds, it is likely to endure. But do be careful how you position this rose for I'm sure that even Wheatcroft would have admitted that there's not much that goes with it. "

FORM
Small, spreading bush.

FLOWERS
Large, double, orange-scarlet with bright yellow stripes and yellow reverses to the petals, slight fragrance.

SPECIAL FEATURES
With colours like this, a rose doesn't need anything else.

SHADE TOLERANCE Light to moderate.
WEATHER TOLERANCE Moderate

'Harry Wheatcroft'

'Crimson Glory'
(Also a climbing form)
(A seedling of 'Cathrine Kordes' x 'W E Chaplin')
[1935, Kordes, Germany]

" This was probably the outstanding red pre-war Hybrid Tea and is still a fine variety today, although there are now several roses that can better it for disease resistance, overall form and constancy of colour. Pretty well all of these defects can be forgiven, however, for its wonderful fragrance. "

FORM
Small, spreading and rather loose bush.

FLOWERS
Large, double, rich velvety red and strong fragrance.

SPECIAL FEATURES
Mildew- and blackspot-prone, not a good rose on poor soils or in hot sun.

'Crimson Glory'

SHADE TOLERANCE Light to moderate.
WEATHER TOLERANCE Poor to moderate.

OTHER RECOMMENDED ROSES
'National Trust' (syn. 'Bad Naukeim') ('Evelyn Fison' x 'King of Hearts') [1970, McGredy, Northern Ireland], a small, upright bush, medium-sized, double, very full crimson flowers in large numbers, no fragrance.
'Uncle Walter' ('Detroiter' x 'Heidelberg') [1963, McGredy, Northern Ireland], a medium-sized upright bush or shrub, medium-sized, double, crimson flowers, slight fragrance, a big, vigorous plant, useful for screening, disease resistant and weather tolerant.
'Château de Clos-Vougeot' (Also a climbing form) (Unknown parentage) [1908, Pernet-Duchet, France], a small, spreading bush, large, velvety deep crimson flowers, strong fragrance; one of the oldest Hybrid Teas still widely available.

HYBRID TEAS (syn. Large-flowered Roses)

'Deep Secret'
(Parentage not disclosed)
[1977, Tantau, Germany]

'Deep Secret'

❝ There are many candidates for the darkest coloured of all roses and this variety is always on the short list, although my own experience is that it falls short of 'Guinée' and even 'Josephine Bruce'. But that doesn't make it any less worthy a plant, for it is possessed of a fine velvety texture and wonderful perfume. ❞

FORM
Small, upright bush.
FLOWERS
Large, double, velvety dark crimson, very fragrant.
SPECIAL FEATURES
Well-shaped flowers, vigorous upright growth and good disease resistance.

SHADE TOLERANCE
Moderate to good.
WEATHER TOLERANCE
Moderate.

'Royal William' ('Feuerzauber' x a seedling)
[1984, Kordes, Germany]

❝ There's much to be said for giving a rose a sentimental or royal name if you want to be certain of a good public response, and this one has proved no exception. This is not to be cynical, however, for it clearly has merits and was voted British Rose of the Year in 1987, no mean achievement for a Hybrid Tea. I would, nonetheless, have preferred it to have more fragrance and it will have to reveal more than good disease resistance to displace some of the older dark reds from my affections. ❞

FORM
Small, upright bush.
FLOWERS
Medium-sized, double, velvety dark red, moderately fragrant.
SPECIAL FEATURES
Well-shaped flowers on a well-shaped plant with healthy foliage; and, of course, that royal connection.

SHADE TOLERANCE
Moderate to good.
WEATHER TOLERANCE
Good.

'Royal William'

'Josephine Bruce'
(Also a climbing form)
('Crimson Glory' x 'Madge Whipp') [1949, Bees, England]

❝ *I had never grown 'Josephine Bruce' until I was sent a plant as a substitute for another, sold-out variety and only then did I realize what I had been missing. Everyone tells me that it is a fussy plant and only gives of its best with much cossetting but I can only voice my personal experience and say that I find it trouble-free and reliable.* ❞

FORM
Small, spreading bush.
FLOWERS
Large, double, velvety dark crimson, very fragrant.

SPECIAL FEATURES
Well-shaped flowers, good disease resistance (in my experience; others tell me that it is mildew-prone, so take your chances).

'Josephine Bruce'

SHADE TOLERANCE
Moderate.
WEATHER TOLERANCE
Moderate .

OTHER RECOMMENDED ROSES

'Ingrid Bergman' (a seedling x a seedling) [1983, Poulsen, Denmark], a small, upright bush, medium-sized, double dark red flowers, moderate fragrance; good disease resistance, good weather tolerance.

'Papa Meilland' ('Chrysler Imperial' x 'Charles Mallerin') [1963, Meilland, France], a small, upright bush, large, dark crimson flowers, strong fragrance; poor disease resistance; needs good growing conditions.

'Ruby Wedding' ('Mayflower' x an unknown variety) [1979, Gregory, England], a small, tidy, spreading bush with medium-sized, double, dark ruby-red flowers, slight fragrance; poor disease resistance but a very popular variety as a gift on certain occasions.

'Blue Moon' (syn. 'Blue Monday', 'Mainzer Fastnacht', 'Sissi') (Also a climbing form) ('Sterling Silver' x an unknown variety) [1964, Tantau, Germany]

'Blue Moon'

❝ *This is it, the closest anyone has come to breeding a blue rose if that is really what you want. In truth, there are old shrub varieties in more attractive shades of lilac, for that is what this really is, but it is a rare colour among Hybrid Teas. Like many flowers of this hue, I find it a very difficult rose to photograph satisfactorily, different films and printing techniques rendering it varyingly close to a proper blue. So be sure you see the real thing rather than a picture, before you decide if you like it.* ❞

FORM
Small, upright bush.
FLOWERS
Medium-sized, double, silver-mauve, strong fragrance.
SPECIAL FEATURES
Poor disease resistance and rather weak growth scarcely seem prices worth paying for the colour.

SHADE TOLERANCE Light to moderate.
WEATHER TOLERANCE
Moderate.

CLIMBING HYBRID TEAS

Far more varieties of bush Hybrid Teas than Floribundas have sported to produce climbing forms and I have indicated in my descriptions of the bush varieties where a climbing form exists. In most instances, however, varieties tend to be much better in one form than the other and only in relatively few instances have I included a detailed description of a rose in both sections. Where two forms occur, the climbing form is denoted by the word 'Climbing' before the variety name, although in nursery catalogues, you will sometimes find it used as a suffix. This convention makes it easy to distinguish the sports of bush varieties from those climbing Hybrid Teas that were bred as, and exist only in, the climbing form, something that I don't think occurs with Floribundas. As with the bush Hybrid Teas, no Hybrid Tea Climbers produce noteworthy hips, most are more or less continuous-flowering and all should be pruned similarly, in this instance by Method 8 (p.25).

'Climbing Mrs Herbert Stevens' ('Frau Karl Druschki' x 'Niphetos') [Bush, 1910, McGredy, Northern Ireland; Climbing 1922, Pernet-Ducher, France]

❝ I treasure 'Mrs Herbert Stevens' in my own garden for the way that she embraces and is entangled with a miniature climber called 'Pompon de Paris' (p.61); they meet half-way across an arch and create a splendid feature. There is much to be said for having a continuous-flowering rose growing in such a way and this one fulfills most of the criteria you are entitled to expect. ❞

FORM
Medium-sized to tall climber.

FLOWERS
Large, double, of very fine form, white, very fragrant.

SPECIAL FEATURES
Mildew-prone and may suffer die-back in hard winters but always happy to recover after pruning. The scent is truly superb and the flowers very shapely. It can cope pretty well with growing in difficult situations.

SHADE TOLERANCE Good.
WEATHER TOLERANCE
Poor to moderate.

'Climbing Mrs Herbert Stevens'

'Meg' (Probably 'Paul's Lemon Pillar' x 'Madame Butterfly') [1954, Gosset, England]

❝ An extraordinary and lovely rose in its flowers, its existence in climbing form only and, in my garden at least, its relatively short flowering period; it really has much more of a repeat- than continuous-flowering habit. ❞

'Meg'

FORM
Small to medium-sized climber.

FLOWERS
Large, single or semi-double, in small clusters, yellowish pink with red-brown stamens, moderate to strong fragrance.

SPECIAL FEATURES
Despite its relatively short stature, an informal rose, best grown through a small tree. Good disease resistance.

SHADE TOLERANCE Light to moderate.
WEATHER TOLERANCE
Moderate.

'Climbing Madame Caroline Testout'
**('Madame de Tartas' x 'Lady Mary Fitzwilliam')
[Bush, 1890, Pernet-Ducher, France; Climbing, 1901, Chauvry, France]**

'Climbing Madame Caroline Testout'

" These days, the name 'Madame Caroline Testout' tends to be encountered when the variety is referred to as the parent of another variety, rather than attached to the original plant itself. This is a great pity as it was once a very popular variety, for its vigour, hardiness and weather tolerance; and also for its flowers that are of a lovely old, unkempt form. "

FORM
Tall climber.

FLOWERS
Large, double, loose and shaggy in the cabbage form so familiar in much older varieties, silvery-pink, very fragrant.

SPECIAL FEATURES
Needs room to show off its charms and one of the best roses that I have seen on a cool, shady wall.

SHADE TOLERANCE Good.
WEATHER TOLERANCE Good.

OTHER RECOMMENDED ROSES

'Paul's Lemon Pillar' ('Frau Karl Druschki' x 'Maréc') [1915, Paul, England], a tall climber, large, double cream-yellow flowers of very fine form, very fragrant, summer.
'Casino' ('Coral Dawn' x 'Buccaneer') [1963, McGredy, Northern Ireland], a medium-sized climber, large, double, rounded, pale pink flowers opening rather loosely, slight fragrance.
'Easlea's Golden Rambler' (Unknown parentage) [1932, Easlea, England], tall, large, double, loose golden-yellow flowers, strong fragrance; one of the

best yellow climbers of any type.
'Breath of Life' ('Red Dandy' x 'Alexander') [1982, Harkness, England], a low climber, large, double, apricot-pink fragrant flowers; very good combination of colour and flower form.
'Climbing Mrs Sam McGredy', (('Donald Macdonald' x 'Golden Emblem') x (a seedling x 'The Queen Alexandra Rose')) [Bush, 1929, McGredy, Northern Ireland; Climbing, 1937, Buisman, Holland], a tall climber, large, double, loose rich

copper-orange flowers, fragrant; much better than the bush form.
'Climbing Lady Sylvia' (Sport from 'Madame Butterfly') [Bush, 1926, Stevens, England; Climbing, 1933], a tall climber, medium-sized, double, pale pink full flowers with yellow base, very fragrant, a superb and vigorous plant.
'Bantry Bay' ('New Dawn' x 'Korona') [1967, McGredy, Northern Ireland], a large, semi-double rich pink flowers, moderate fragrance, good disease resistance.

CLIMBING HYBRID TEAS

'Madame Grégoire Staechelin' (syn. 'Spanish Beauty') ('Frau Karl Druschki' x 'Chateau de Clos Vougeot') [1927, Dot, Spain]

❝ The Spanish rose breeder Pedro Dot produced relatively few enduring varieties but among them are some quite superb plants. The shrub rose 'Nevada' (p.72) is one; this is another. It is a big, vigorous rose for a big situation; but it requires space for the additional reason that it normally has a single, if magnificent, flush of flowers. So big a plant with such a brief period of glory really would be too much of a luxury in all except large gardens. ❞

FORM
Tall climber.

FLOWERS
Large, semi-double, shell-pink with darker reverse sides, very fragrant.

SPECIAL FEATURES
The overall vigour and wonderful flowers must be weighed up against the short flowering period. Good disease resistance for a variety of this age and, in most years, the additional and unusual bonus of a very good display of large orange-red hips in autumn.

SHADE TOLERANCE
Moderate to good.
WEATHER TOLERANCE
Moderate.

'Madame Grégoire Staechelin'

'Guinée' ('Souvenir de Claudius Denoyel' x 'Ami Quinard') [1938, Mallerin, France]

❝ I failed in my first attempt to obtain 'Guinée', since the nursery was out of stock and sent the climbing form of 'Josephine Bruce' as a substitute. I'm glad I persevered for while 'Josephine Bruce' is a good rose, it simply can't match the incredible deep intensity of the flowers of 'Guinée' itself. There may be darker coloured roses but I have never seen one, and to grow this in the company of plants that have fresh green foliage is a very special delight. ❞

FORM
Medium-sized to tall climber.

FLOWERS
Medium-sized to large, double, deep velvety crimson, very fragrant.

SPECIAL FEATURES
The dark intensity of the flowers is undoubtedly the main reason that this rose is grown, but it also has good disease resistance. It is a vigorous grower if given good conditions in which to grow. Ideally it should be given a sheltered, warm position.

SHADE TOLERANCE
Light to moderate.
WEATHER TOLERANCE
Moderate.

'Guinée'

'Climbing Eden Rose' ('Peace' x 'Signora')
[Bush, 1953, Meilland, France; Climbing, 1962, Meilland, France]

" *This is another rose redolent of my childhood garden. We only grew the climbing form, although neighbours had bushes and indeed won prizes in the Hybrid Tea classes at the village show. But it is the image of the climber embracing an old garden shed that stays with me to this day and although relatively few nurseries now stock it, it is the old climbing Hybrid Tea variety, along with 'Home Sweet Home', I would most like to see regain its popularity.* "

FORM
Tall climber.

FLOWERS
Large, double, rich rose-pink flowers with a hint of silver, moderate fragrance.

SPECIAL FEATURES
A very vigorous variety and one to plant in a featured, central spot in the garden, good disease resistance.

SHADE TOLERANCE Good.
WEATHER TOLERANCE Good.

'Climbing Ena Harkness'
('Crimson Glory' x 'Southport') [Bush, 1946, Norman, England; Climbing, 1954, Murrell, England]

" *Sometimes, gardeners find themselves owing a particular debt to a previous owner of their garden. I owe a special one to a predecessor who planted 'Ena Harkness' against the front wall of my house where she delights visitors to this day. Judging by the apparent age of the plant, it must have been acquired soon after the variety was introduced but while companions (currently and very effectively* Clematis *'Frances Rivis') have come and gone, dear old Ena soldiers on. I'm also amazed at the vigour of the old girl for every two or three years, she throws up a massive, healthy new stem from the base.* "

FORM
Tall climber.

FLOWERS
Large, double, deep velvety crimson, very fragrant.

SPECIAL FEATURES
The flowers have rather weak stems and so the heads have a tendency to hang down, something of a disadvantage in a bush but a positive benefit on a tall wall where the blooms look down at you as you gaze upwards. Good disease resistance.

SHADE TOLERANCE Very good.
WEATHER TOLERANCE Good.

OTHER RECOMMENDED ROSES

'Coral Dawn' ('New Dawn' x (an unknown Hybrid Tea x a Polyantha seedling)) [1952, Boerner, Germany], medium-sized climber, medium-sized coral-pink flowers, only slight fragrance which is a drawback but a good rose of this colour.

'Leaping Salmon' (('Vesper' x 'Aloha') x ('Paddy McGredy' x 'Maigold') x 'Prima Ballerina') [1986, Pearce, England], a medium-sized climber, large, double, salmon-pink flowers, slight fragrance; a less vigorous alternative to 'Coral Dawn' of similar colour.

'Climbing Shot Silk' (Seedling of 'Hugh Dickson' x 'Sunstar') [Bush, 1924, Dickson, Northern Ireland; Climbing 1931, Knight, Australia], a tall climber, medium-sized uniquely coloured rich cerise-pink flowers with orange flush and yellow bases to petals, very fragrant, only moderate disease resistance but there is nothing else of this colour.

'Allen Chandler' ('Hugh Dickson' x a seedling) [1923, Chandler, USA], a medium-sized to tall, large or very large semi-double crimson flowers with obvious gold-yellow stamens, fragrant and disease resistant; one of the most reliable red climbers.

'Climbing Etoile de Hollande' ('General MacArthur' x 'Hadley') [Bush, 1919, Verschuren, Holland'; Climbing 1931, Leenders, Holland], a medium-sized to tall climber, medium-sized double rich, dark crimson flowers, very fragrant, a floriferous, superbly coloured old rose. Disease-prone and summer-flowering only.

MODERN CLIMBERS

A Modern Climber is, literally, a Climbing Rose bred in recent times, although this is one of the most nebulous of the rose groupings. By and large, most Modern Climbers differ from older climbers in that they resemble tall, lax shrubs. This said, they also differ from the climbing sports of Hybrid Teas and Floribundas which tend to produce very long, pliable shoots. There are several varieties, however, which could easily be classed either as Modern Climbers or as Climbing Hybrid Teas and may be found under either category depending on the catalogue. But one important feature of most Modern Climbers is that they have a repeat- or more or less continuous-flowering habit and this certainly sets them apart from most older climbers. All roses in this group should be pruned by Method 7 (p.24).

'Handel' ('Columbine' x 'Heidelberg') [1956, McGredy, Northern Ireland]

❝ *Oddly enough, this has become one of the most famous and popular of all of the roses to come from McGredy's Northern Ireland nursery. I say oddly because the more or less picotee flowers really are an acquired taste. It is a proper candy-floss rose and while I find flowers of this type just about acceptable on a small plant, an entire wall covered with them is a bit much. But many gardeners evidently love it and it is very reliable and certainly unique.* ❞

FORM
Medium-sized to tall climber.
FLOWERS
Large, semi-double, cream-white with pink edges, slight fragrance.
SPECIAL FEATURES
Susceptibility to disease and considerable vigour are features to be aware of. The leaves are a glossy green and show off the flowers to a great effect. The markings on the flowers seem to get deeper as the rose ages.

'Handel'

SHADE TOLERANCE None to light.
WEATHER TOLERANCE Moderate.

'Golden Showers' ('Charlotte Armstrong' x 'Captain Thomas') [1956, Lammerts, USA]

❝ *Ask a number of gardening experts for a reliable, none-too-vigorous yellow Climbing Rose and the chances are that the majority will opt for 'Golden Showers'. I think I would be among them, although I should add that this is because there is no really outstanding rose of this type and this is simply the best available.* ❞

FORM
Low to medium-sized climber.
FLOWERS
Large, double, golden-yellow but soon fading to yellow-cream, slightly fragrant.
SPECIAL FEATURES
Good disease resistance for a yellow rose and a long flowering season.

SHADE TOLERANCE
Moderate to almost deep.
WEATHER TOLERANCE
Good.

'Golden Showers'

'Maigold' ('Poulsen's Pink' x 'Fruhlingstag') [1953, Kordes, Germany]

❝ When 'Maigold' is in flower, I know that spring has truly arrived. It vies with Rosa primula *and 'Canary Bird' for the privilege of being the earliest-flowering rose in most parts of England and, not surprisingly, they all come from fairly closely related ancestors. It is a remarkably lovely variety but always bear in mind that its flowering period is short. It does not have the repeat-flowering characteristic of Modern Climbers. ❞*

FORM

Medium-sized climber.

FLOWERS

Large, semi-double, rich golden-yellow with gold stamens, strong fragrance.

SPECIAL FEATURES

The early spring-flowering is of course the overriding virtue of this rose but the colour is very strong, the stems extremely strong and thorny, and disease resistance very good. Because of the thorns don't place close to a path.

SHADE TOLERANCE

Moderate to almost deep.

WEATHER TOLERANCE

Moderate to good.

'Swan Lake'

OTHER RECOMMENDED ROSES

'Swan Lake' ('Memoriam' x 'Heidelberg') [1968, McGredy, Northern Ireland], a low climber, large, double white fragrant flowers with slight pink flush, good weather tolerance but rather disease-prone. 'White Cockade' ('New Dawn' x 'Circus') [1969, Cocker, Scotland], a low climber, beautifully formed medium-sized, double white flowers, slight fragrance, good disease-resistance and weather tolerance. 'Leverkusen' (Rosa x kordesii x 'Golden Glow') [1954, Kordes, Germany], low to medium-sized climber, large, double, cream-yellow flowers, moderate fragrance. 'Lawrence Johnston' (syn. 'Hidcote Yellow') ('Madame Eugène Verdier' x Rosa foetida persiana) [1923, Pernet-Ducher, France], a tall or very tall climber, large, semi-double, loose bright yellow flowers, very fragrant, mainly early summer-flowering and very floriferous. A fine rose but prone to blackspot. 'Royal Gold' ('Goldilocks' x 'Lydia') [1957, Morey, USA], a low climber, large, well-formed, double deep yellow flowers, slight fragrance; needs some shelter and good growing conditions.

'Maigold'

MODERN CLIMBERS

'Schoolgirl' ('Coral Dawn' x 'Belle Blonde') [1964, McGredy, Northern Ireland]

" *I used to think that I was alone in wondering why 'Schoolgirl' was so popular but recently I've come to realize that many rose specialists share this view, although their nurseries continue to supply it to, presumably, a contented public. The flowers are a pleasing enough colour and it may be that there is nothing better of this shade on offer. In my view, however, its growth will always be relatively poor and this seems to me a classic opportunity for someone to breed a rose of this colour but with better vigour.* "

SPECIAL FEATURES
The colour is interesting but do give this rose the best possible conditions; the foliage tends to be rather thin and blackspot-prone.

FORM
Low to medium-sized climber.

FLOWERS
Large, double copper-orange, rather sparse, very fragrant.

SHADE TOLERANCE Light.
WEATHER TOLERANCE Moderate.

'School Girl'

'Danse du Feu' ('Paul's Scarlet' x a seedling of *Rosa multiflora*) [1953, Mallerin, France]

" *If you want a rose to set your garden ablaze, then the appropriately named 'Danse du Feu' is it, a flower of truly viciously fiery colour. If you like this effect, then certainly there is nothing else (pardon the expression) to hold a candle to it. When you are deciding where to plant this rose bear in mind that other plants in your garden (and, indeed, even the bricks of your house itself) will also have to be taken into account and their colours just might not blend.* "

'Danse du Feu'

FORM
Low climber.

FLOWERS
Medium-sized, double, vivid orange-scarlet, little or no fragrance.

SPECIAL FEATURES
The colour, lurid as it is, does fade but not especially attractively to become a sort of insipid plum and, in most summers, mildew will be a problem.

SHADE TOLERANCE
Moderate to almost deep.
WEATHER TOLERANCE
Moderate to good.

'Aloha' ('Mercedes Gallart' x 'New Dawn') [1949, Boerner, USA]

❝ I think that 'Aloha' probably spans the boundary between shrubs and low climbers almost better than any other variety, and I really don't mind how you grow it, but grow it you must. I have gone into print several times saying that I consider it almost the perfect modern rose, a statement I stand by. It seems to me to have all the virtues that today's gardener wants from a rose and, even in a very small garden, it makes a perfect pillar specimen. ❞

FORM
Low climber.
FLOWERS
Medium-sized to large, double, rich rose-pink, strong fragrance.
SPECIAL FEATURES
Disease and, in my experience, pest resistance, the foliage, fragrance, colour and limited size make a perfect blend.

SHADE TOLERANCE
Moderate.
WEATHER TOLERANCE
Good.

'Aloha'

OTHER RECOMMENDED ROSES
'Laura Ford' (Parentage not disclosed) [1989, Warner, England], a low climber, small, double yellow-orange flowers, slight or no fragrance. Almost a Miniature Climber, and like all Miniatures, in need of extra care and attention. 'Warm Welcome' (Parentage not disclosed) [1990, Warner, England], a low Climber, small, orange-vermillion flowers, no fragrance; like 'Laura Ford' a Miniature variety and from the same English stable. 'Constance Spry' ('Belle Isis' x 'Dainty Maid') [1960, Austin, England], a low to medium-sized climber, very large, double, strongly fragrant clear pink flowers; a beautiful rose that may also be grown as a shrub. The forerunner of the English Roses (p.76) but rather mildew-prone. 'Morning Jewel' ('New Dawn' x 'Red Dandy') [1968, Cocker, Scotland], a low to medium-sized climber, medium-sized, double, vivid pink flowers, slightly fragrant.

'Pink Perpétué' ('Danse du Feu' x 'New Dawn') [1965, Gregory, England]

❝ A remarkable combination of parents has produced the genuinely hybrid flowers of this rose. The soft pink of 'New Dawn' has tamed the fire of 'Danse du Feu' to yield a shade that is a real blend; pink but with a warm heart. I've seen it described as harsh but I think assertive is closer to the mark. ❞

FORM
Medium-sized to tall climber.
FLOWERS
Medium-sized, double, rich rose-pink, in large numbers, moderate fragrance.
SPECIAL FEATURES
In some gardens I'm reliably told rust can be a problem but I've only ever seen it on my plant in very wet summers.

'Pink Perpétué'

SHADE TOLERANCE
Moderate.
WEATHER TOLERANCE
Good.

MODERN CLIMBERS

'Compassion'
('White Cockade' x 'Prima Ballerina')
[1973, Harkness, England]

" *This rose has been in demand since its introduction and this could be due to a number of factors: the colour, the number and form of the flowers, the fragrance. So why is it that when I have tried it, mildew has been its downfall? Grow it as a pillar rose rather than a climber, for a more open situation would reduce the likelihood of disease.* "

FLOWERS
Large, double, salmon-pink with a hint of orange, very fragrant.

SPECIAL FEATURES
Take your pick because I believe that this may be the biggest-selling of all Climbing Roses.

FORM
Low climber.

SHADE TOLERANCE Light.
WEATHER TOLERANCE Moderate to good.

'Compassion'

'Dream Girl' ('Dr W Van Fleet' x 'Senora Gari')
[1944, Bobbink, USA]

" *To be honest, 'Dream Girl' must by now be Dream Woman and a bit old to be considered modern but I'm not sure where else to place her. It is a variety that must feature in anyone's list of climbers, for the flowers have that flattened, rosette-like shape so characteristic of many old roses but rather a rarity among those of today.* "

SHADE TOLERANCE Light.
WEATHER TOLERANCE Moderate to good.

FORM
Low climber.

FLOWERS
Small to medium, double, neat, gentle coral-pink, strong and very distinctive fragrance, flowers mid- to late summer.

SPECIAL FEATURES
Disease resistance is good for a variety of this age although the flowering period is rather limited.

'Hamburger Phoenix'

'Dortmund'

'Dublin Bay' ('Bantry Bay' x 'Altissimo') [1976, McGredy, Northern Ireland]

❝ *Over the years the McGredy nursery has produced a number of climbers named after Irish bays but this is my, and most other people's, favourite; although one of its parents, 'Altissimo', is another contender. To my mind it is easily the best pillar rose of its colour; and an isolated pillar is really the most appropriate place to grow it for it isn't easy to combine with other colours nearby. This will also ensure the presence of an arresting feature in the garden.* ❞

FORM
Low climber.

FLOWERS
Medium-sized, double, rich red, with a slight fragrance.

SPECIAL FEATURES
Good disease resistance and a very long and reliable flowering season.

SHADE TOLERANCE Light to moderate.

WEATHER TOLERANCE Good.

'Dublin Bay'

OTHER RECOMMENDED ROSES

'Altissimo' ('Tenor' x unknown variety) [1966, Delbard-Chabert, France], a medium-sized climber, large, single, rich red flowers with gold stamens, no fragrance. Like others of this type, distinctive but hard to position correctly.

'Parade' (seedling of 'New Dawn' x 'World's Fair') [1953, Boerner, USA], a low climber, large, double, rich cerise-pink flowers, strong fragrance, good disease resistance and weather tolerance – and a long flowering period.

'Dortmund' (a seedling x *Rosa* x *kordesii*) [1955, Kordes, Germany] a low climber, large, single, crimson flowers with white central 'eye', slight fragrance; good disease resistance and the advantage of moderate shade tolerance.

'Hamburger Phoenix' (*Rosa* x *kordesii* x a seedling) [1954, Kordes, Germany], a low climber, large, semi-double, rich crimson flowers, moderate fragrance and the bonus of attractive orange-red hips.

'Parkdirektor Riggers' (*Rosa* x *kordesii* x 'Our Princess') [1954, Kordes, Germany]

❝ *I've always puzzled over what kind of contribution the eponymous Parkdirektor could have made to be immortalized in so distinctive a fashion, for it really is a rather ungainly name. The variety certainly isn't ungainly but it is a rose of a type that I would not normally grow: those violently-coloured, almost single flowers being difficult to place satisfactorily. Since I found a sunny spot against a pale-coloured wall, however, I have grown it for several years with great pleasure.* ❞

'Parkdirektor Riggers'

SPECIAL FEATURES
There is a special charm about single-flowered climbers. And while, officially, classed as semi-double they have few enough petals to satisfy my criteria.

SHADE TOLERANCE Light.

WEATHER TOLERANCE Good.

FORM
Medium-sized climber.

FLOWERS
Medium-sized, almost single, in large clusters, velvety red, slight fragrance.

RAMBLERS

The very name Rambler seems to sum up what, for many people, are the outstanding characteristics of old rose varieties: beautiful disorder, a casual informality, and, for the more cynical, mildew. Yes, everyone has heard of Ramblers yet not one gardener in ten could tell you the difference between a Rambler and a Climber; and very few realize that, as a group, the Ramblers really aren't so very old. Ramblers are best described in terms of their obvious characteristics: they have long, often very long, pliable shoots, they flower almost exclusively in the early summer and generally produce very large numbers of individually rather small flowers.

   This definition could include a few roses that I have placed elsewhere, but it embraces the varieties derived from two Oriental rose species, *Rosa multiflora* and *R. wichuraiana*. These were introduced to Britain in 1862 and 1891 respectively which is relatively recent in rose history. These species were crossed at the turn of the century, during the Edwardian period, and later with Hybrid Perpetuals, Tea Roses and Hybrid Teas. In general, the Multiflora Ramblers have larger and fewer flowers, less pliable stems and often grow taller than the Wichuraiana types but Ramblers are all essentially informal roses. They are not ideally suited to being restricted in limited space, and it is a matter of great sadness to many rose growers that so few Ramblers now remain, having been ousted in favour of the even wider colour range, tamer habit and generally much longer flowering period of the Modern Climbers. I would love to think that more gardeners would welcome them back. Pruning varies, depending on the parentage of the variety.

'Bobbie James'
(Unknown parentage; Multiflora type)
[1961, Sunningdale Nurseries, England]

❝ This is a real rarity, a modern Rambler, and although its parentage remains a mystery, it has the characteristics of all the great Multiflora Ramblers of the past. It has, in fact, become so much a part of the rose-growing world that it seems incredible to many gardeners that this it is such a new variety. It is, in most ways, almost the perfect rambling rose, extremely vigorous with masses of small, very fragrant and perfectly formed flowers. How gardeners from the Edwardian period would have loved it. ❞

FORM
Tall rambler.

FLOWERS
Small, semi-double blooms of lovely cup-like shape, white with yellow stamens, held in enormous clusters and a very strong fragrance.

HIPS
Small, oval, orange.

SPECIAL FEATURES
If you want a big, white rambler, you really need look no further; and even the disease resistance is pretty good.

SHADE TOLERANCE
Moderate to almost deep.
WEATHER TOLERANCE
Moderate to good.
PRUNING – 6

'Bobbie James'

'Rambling Rector'
[Unknown origin; Multiflora type]

❝ *No-one knows which rector rambled or how long ago he did it but this is another typical Multiflora variety with slightly less pliable stems than the Wichuraiana types. It has much in common with 'Bobbie James', see previous page, and would be short-listed by most rose growers' as a variety able to cover unsightly old buildings and other obtrusive structures in the most picturesque fashion.* ❞

'Albéric Barbier'
(*Rosa wichuraiana* x 'Shirley Hibberd') [1921, Barbier, France]

❝ *One of the half-dozen or so most popular of the surviving old Ramblers and probably the best near-white among the Wichuraiana varieties. But if you grow it, don't fall into my mistake of forgetting that, despite the parentage, it can be a very vigorous rose. I planted mine close to an old white-painted lean-to greenhouse which I thought would complement its colour. It did, but only for a season or two after which it swallowed the greenhouse whole.* ❞

SHADE TOLERANCE
Moderate to almost deep.
WEATHER TOLERANCE
Moderate to good.
PRUNING – 5

FORM
Tall rambler.
FLOWERS
Small, semi-double, cream then becoming white, with yellow stamens, in large clusters, moderate to strong fragrance.
HIPS
Small, oval, orange.
SPECIAL FEATURES
Disease resistance isn't good. If space is available grow it as a free-standing mound because of the dense habit.

'Albéric Barbier'

FORM
Tall rambler.
FLOWERS
Medium-sized to large, double, cream, in small clusters, very fragrant.
HIPS
None.
SPECIAL FEATURES
Among the best mildew resistance among Wichuraiana varieties and there is really nothing else as good with flowers of this colour and size.

'Rambling rector'

SHADE TOLERANCE
Moderate to almost deep.
WEATHER TOLERANCE
Moderate to good.
PRUNING – 6

OTHER RECOMMENDED ROSES
'Sanders' White Rambler' (syn. 'Sanders' White') (Unknown parentage; Multiflora type) [1912, Sanders, England], a tall Rambler, small, semi-double white flowers in large clusters, strong fragrance; flowers later than many Ramblers, good shade tolerance. Pruning 6.
'Seagull' (Unknown parentage; Multiflora type) [1907, Pritchard, England], a tall Rambler, small, semi-double white flowers with yellow stamens in very large clusters; a wonderful plant, given room and good conditions. Pruning 6.
'Emily Gray' ('Jersey Beauty' x 'Comtesse du Cayla'; Multiflora type) [1918, Williams, England], a medium-sized to tall Rambler, medium-sized, semi-double lemon-yellow flowers, moderate fragrance; lovely but not very hardy so best in sheltered conditions. Pruning 6.

RAMBLERS

'Goldfinch' ('Hélène' x an unknown variety; Multiflora type) [1907, Paul, England]

66 I always think this a very modern name for a rose of its period but I'm sure that the colour, which is unusual for any Multiflora and especially unusual at that time, persuaded William Paul that it needed something striking. It is a good Rambler for a small garden because of its limited vigour. 99

FORM
Low to medium-sized Rambler.

FLOWERS
Small, semi-double, pale yellow-apricot of very neat shape, yellow stamens, moderate fragrance.

HIPS
None.

SPECIAL FEATURES
Apart from the size and colour, there is an added attribute that suits 'Goldfinch' for a small space in that it is almost thornless. Disease resistance is only moderate in my garden.

SHADE TOLERANCE
Moderate.

WEATHER TOLERANCE
Moderate.

PRUNING – 6

'Goldfinch'

'New Dawn' (Sport from 'Dr W Van Fleet'; Wichuraiana type) [1930, Somerset Rose Company, USA]

66 This remarkable rose must be the most widely planted Rambler at the time of writing; although not many people realize that this is the case as nurseries tend to sell it under the category of Climber. This probably explains why it is the single variety about which I receive the greatest number of pruning queries. If its origins were better known, its pruning would seem logical. It is less vigorous than the parent which it has all but replaced, but the outstanding virtue that ensures immortality for the Somerset Rose Company, and which is why it is so often called a Climber, is that it is repeat-flowering. 99

FORM
Medium-sized rambler.

FLOWERS
Medium-sized, semi-double to double, soft pink, very fragrant.

HIPS
None.

SPECIAL FEATURES
Good disease resistance for a Rambler. Recommended for hedging but I don't find its shade tolerance good enough for this purpose. Repeat-flowering.

SHADE TOLERANCE Light to moderate.

WEATHER TOLERANCE
Moderate to good.

PRUNING – 5

'New Dawn'

'Dorothy Perkins' (*Rosa wichuraiana* x 'Madame Gabriel Luizet') [1901, Jackson & Perkins, USA]

" A rose with a chain of women's clothing shops named after it is already well on the way to a place in history. But the beauty of 'Dorothy Perkins' is more than just underwear deep, for it has an enduring place in many gardeners' affections by virtue of its most unusual pink colour. And so charming is this that we are willing to forgive the mildew that it is prone to and the demanding conditions needed, for this is not an easy rose to grow well. "

FORM
Medium-sized to tall Rambler.

FLOWERS
Small, semi-double to double, rich pink, very fragrant.

HIPS
None.

SPECIAL FEATURES
Must have good soil, and a sheltered and slightly cool, ventilated position – on a large tripod in a moist border is ideal. Sadly, very prone to mildew although when grown as I have suggested this is, at least, containable.

'Dorothy Perkins'

SHADE TOLERANCE None to light.
WEATHER TOLERANCE Poor to moderate.
PRUNING – 5

'Albertine' (*Rosa wichuraiana* x 'Mrs Arthur Robert Waddell') [1921, Barbier, France]

" I would guess that this is the best-known of all Ramblers, although certainly not the best variety; it has far too many defects. Its reputation rests mainly on an appealing colour although a rather long-flowering period helps too. But, for me, once again, it was mildew that finally caused me to banish it from my garden. "

FORM
Medium-sized to tall Rambler.

FLOWERS
Large, double, copper-pink, with a strong fragrance.

HIPS
None.

SPECIAL FEATURES
The flowers are of fine form and large for a Rambler but the mildew is large and fine too. In truth, there are Modern Climbers of similar colour that are available that would be a much better choice for growing in a small garden.

SHADE TOLERANCE None to light.
WEATHER TOLERANCE Moderate.
PRUNING – 5

OTHER RECOMMENDED ROSES
'Phyllis Bide' ('Perle d'Or' x 'Gloire de Dijon') [1923, Bide, England], a medium-sized Rambler, small, irregular, semi-double very pale yellow and pink flowers, moderate fragrance, reliably repeat flowering; a pretty and useful rose. Pruning 6.
'Paul Transon' (*Rosa wichuraiana* x 'l'Idéale') [1900, Barbier, France], a medium-sized to tall Rambler, medium-sized, double, copper-pink and yellow flowers, moderate fragrance; must have good conditions when it will be reliably repeat-flower. Pruning 5.
'Chaplin's Pink Climber' (syn. 'Chaplin's Pink') ('Paul's Scarlet' x 'American Pillar'; Wichuraiana type) [1928, Chaplin Bros, England], a tall, medium-sized, semi-double vivid pink flowers, yellow stamens, moderate fragrance. Pruning 5.

'Albertine'

RAMBLERS

'American pillar'

'American Pillar' ((*Rosa wichuraiana* x *Rosa setigera*) x a red Hybrid Perpetual)) [1902, Van Fleet, USA]

❝ You won't walk past 'American Pillar' without noticing, for this is one of the most assertive of roses and must be the most assertive Rambler. There isn't anything else quite like it and it is one of those varieties that divides gardeners' opinions. One nurseryman tells me that he still sells dozens while another says that its popularity has dropped, something I find surprising as some of the biggest selling modern Floribundas have flowers that are no less arresting. ❞

SHADE TOLERANCE
Moderate.
WEATHER TOLERANCE
Good.
PRUNING – 5

FORM
Medium-sized to tall Rambler.
FLOWERS
Medium-sized, single, vivid red-pink with white centres in large clusters, little or no fragrance.
HIPS
None.
SPECIAL FEATURES
With a bicolour such as this, there's no need to look for anything else; you either want it or you don't.

'Crimson shower'

'Crimson Shower' (A seedling of 'Excelsa') [1951, Norman, England]

❝ I have always rated this relatively recent variety the best red Rambler. Admittedly, the competition isn't enormous, for there are rather few that can approach its intensity but given the right situation (by which I mean not against a red brick wall), a large well established plant in full cry is an eye-catching feature in the garden. But do watch that positioning carefully: there is no doubt that it looks best when grown against grey or white. ❞

FORM
Medium-sized to tall Rambler.
FLOWERS
Small, rather neat and rosette-like, double, vivid crimson coloured flowers, slight fragrance.
HIPS
None.
SPECIAL FEATURES
Good disease resistance and with fresh, dark green foliage that admirably sets off the fiery flowers. But never underestimate just how hot and fiery they are and do think carefully before planting.

SHADE TOLERANCE
Moderate.
WEATHER TOLERANCE
Good.
PRUNING – 6

'Paul's Scarlet Climber' ('Paul's Carmine Pillar' x 'Rêve d'Or'; Multiflora type) [1915, Paul, England]

❝ No-one, including William Paul himself, it seems, really knew whether this is a Rambler or a Climber but it does have all of the characteristics of a Multiflora Rambler and that is how I treat it. It's one of those seemingly anonymous red roses that I find rather commonly in old and neglected cottage gardens, testimony to a popularity in years gone by. It isn't an especially popular rose at the time of writing because there are modern repeat-flowering reds but it's still not a bad plant if you want to recreate an old cottage garden feel. ❞

FORM
Medium-sized Rambler.
FLOWERS
Small, semi-double, bright scarlet, very slight fragrance.
HIPS
None.
SPECIAL FEATURES
A good old-fashioned rose although disease resistance is good for its age.

SHADE TOLERANCE
Moderate.
WEATHER TOLERANCE
Good.
PRUNING – 6

'Paul's Scarlet Climber'

'Violette' (Unknown parentage; Multiflora type) [1921, Turbat, France]

❝ There is a small group of purple-flowered Ramblers of which I think this the best, followed closely by 'Veilchenblau', see Other Recommended Roses. It's surprising, nonetheless, how frequently this colour is depicted in paintings of old rose gardens and I can only conclude that it was once a very popular specimen. I find that all of these purple varieties tend to fade in hot sun and so one of my reasons for picking 'Violette' is that it has better shade tolerance, and also better disease resistance than many of the other varieties available. I would like to see this Rambler grown more widely. ❞

FORM
Medium-sized to tall Rambler.
FLOWERS
Small, double, cup-shaped, red-purple with an unusual slight yellow flush, moderate fragrance.
HIPS
None.
SPECIAL FEATURES
The colour blends wonderfully with some of the soft pink varieties.

SHADE TOLERANCE
Moderate.
WEATHER TOLERANCE
Good.
PRUNING – 6

OTHER RECOMMENDED ROSES

'François Juranville' (*Rosa wichuraiana* x 'Madame Laurette Messimy') [1906, Barbier, France], a tall Rambler, medium-sized, double, markedly irregular bright rose-pink flowers, moderate fragrance; the flowers are unique but it is rather prone to mildew. Pruning 5.

'Excelsa' (syn. 'Red Dorothy Perkins') (Unknown parentage; Wichuraiana type) [1909, Walsh, USA], a tall Rambler, small, double, crimson flowers with paler centres; rather prone to mildew but a good old rose. Pruning 5.

'Veilchenblau' (syn. 'Violet Blue') ('Crimson Rambler' x 'Erinnerung an Brod'; Multiflora type) [1909, Schmidt, Germany], a tall rambler, small, double, cup-shaped violet flowers, fading to pale mauve, moderate fragrance; rather mildew-prone. Pruning 6.

INDEX

INDEX/PHOTOGRAPHIC ACKNOWLEDGEMENTS

Front cover: Clive Nichols, The Anchorage, Kent **Back cover (inset):** Professor Stefan Buczacki

Inside photographs

Professor Stefan Buczacki 12, 14, 28 top, 32, 67, 68 bottom, 73 top, 74, 80 right, 98 top, 101 bottom, 101 top, 103 top, 110 centre, 117 right, 119 centre; Eric Crichton 9, 38 left, 40, 54 right, 65 top, 72 right, 90 top, 93 centre, 114 right, 119 top, 120; John Fielding 66, 72 left, 110 right, 115 bottom; Garden Picture Library /David Askham 78 bottom, /David Askham, Lackham College, Wiltshire 68 top, 100 left, /Brian Carter 11, /Densey Clyne 105 centre, /John Glover 116 bottom, /Sunniva Harte, The Old Parsonage, Kent (National Gardens Scheme) 75 bottom, /Mayer/Le Scanff 18 bottom, /Jerry Pavia 118 bottom right, /Howard Rice, Courtesy of Harkness New Roses, Hitchin 91 top, /Brigitte Thomas 13, /Mel Watson 19 left, /Steven Wooster 19 right, 22; John Glover 15, 34 bottom, 42 bottom, 43 left, 51 bottom, 58 right, 77 bottom, 84, 97 top, 123 bottom, 124 right; Harkness New Roses, Hitchin 88 bottom; Jerry Harpur /David Austin Roses, Albrighton 6, /Peckover House, Wisbech 1; Andrew Lawson 21, 52, 57 left, 58 left, 60, 63, 105 bottom, 114 left, 122 bottom, 124 left; Clive Nichols 47, /The Anchorage, Kent 45 top; Photos Horticultural 26 top, 27 right, 27 left, 33 top, 34 top, 36, 39, 41 bottom, 42 top, 43 right, 46 top, 49, 53 bottom, 55 top, 55 bottom, 62, 70, 71 top, 76 left, 77 top, 79, 81 top, 81 bottom, 83 top, 85 right, 92, 93 left, 93 right, 94, 95 bottom, 99 left, 100 right, 102 top, 102 bottom, 103 centre, 104 bottom, 106 bottom, 107 top, 108 top, 108 bottom, 111, 112 bottom, 112 top, 115 top, 116 top, 118 centre bottom, 121 centre, 125; Reed International Books Ltd 18 top, 57 right, /Sue Atkinson 17, /W F Davidson 96 top, /Michael Warren 7, /Steven Wooster 51 top, 61, 65 bottom, 83 bottom, 85 left, 87 bottom, 91 bottom, 96 bottom, 97 bottom, 117 centre, 118 top, 122 top; Royal National Rose Society 99 centre; Harry Smith Collection 10, 20, 26 bottom left, 26 bottom right, 28 bottom, 29 bottom, 29 top, 33 bottom, 37, 38 right, 41 top, 44, 45 bottom, 46 bottom, 48, 53 top, 54 left, 56, 59, 64, 69, 71 bottom, 73 bottom, 75 top, 75 centre, 76 right, 78 top, 80 left, 82 top, 82 bottom, 86 top, 86 right, 87 right, 88 top, 89 top, 89 bottom, 90 bottom, 95 top, 98 bottom right, 98 centre bottom, 104 top, 106 top, 107 bottom, 109 bottom, 109 centre, 121 top, 123 top.

The complete range of books in the 'Best' series is available from all good bookshops or by Mail Order direct from the publisher. Phone through your order on our special CREDIT CARD HOTLINE on 01933 410511.